Iconic Leadership: Forging a New Path to Employee Inspiration

Inspiring Leadership in a Changing World

By: Mustafa Nejem

Table of Content

Introduction to the Book

Today, businesses in the fast-paced and ever-changing world of today are no longer traditional approaches to leadership. The role of leaders has changed greatly, and a new kind of leadership is needed that can inspire and motivate employees in today's workplace.

One of the main challenges facing leaders in this age and time is how to adapt within the changing dynamics of work. Remote working is now becoming popular, meaning that leaders have to come up with innovative ways of engaging their teams from a distance. Also, there are more diverse teams today as seen in terms of both culture and skill sets. This kind of diversity brings new perspectives and opportunities for innovation but also calls for adaptability and inclusiveness from leaders.

Still, employees' expectations have been drastically altered over time. Employees now want not just work but meaningful jobs that accord with their principles while making a difference. They value transparency, open communication, and having a sense of purpose at work. Leaders must therefore recognize these changing expectations so that they can create environments in which inspiration and motivation can be fostered.

Henceforth, iconic leadership has emerged as a viable remedy within this environment. Iconic leaders know it is important to deeply connect with members of their team thereby inspiring them into achieving great things. They go beyond traditional leadership methods even as they exhibit qualities such as authenticity, vision and emotional intelligence among many others. As such, they become role models who can ignite the passion and drive within their employees.

In this book we will explore the transformative power associated with iconic leadership. We shall look at different aspects relating leadership psychology such as theories and concepts behind employee inspiration or motivation among other factors. Additionally, we shall provide practical strategies together with actionable advice that may assist readers develop their own iconic leadership style.

Becoming an iconic leader is accompanied by some obstacles along the way. It calls for self-reflection, resilience in addition to confronting one's own limitations. However, these challenges often teach us valuable lessons as we experience self-discovery and personal growth, which will not only make us great leaders but also role models of influence.

In this journey together, let's embrace a changing landscape of leadership and commit ourselves to forging a new path towards employee inspiration. In this way, we will create positive and empowering work environments that allow people to flourish and develop their full potential. Traditional approaches to leadership in organizations have been largely based on autocratic leadership styles where leaders rely on hierarchical structures and top down decision making. They may have served well enough in the past but they are increasingly being realized to be ineffective as the workplace is rapidly changing today.

One of the major weaknesses of traditional leadership approaches is that they tend to discourage employee engagement and creativity. Autocratic style leaders make decisions with minimal input from their team members leading to lack of ownership and buy-in. This can result in reduced motivation levels thus causing an indifferent workforce thereby impacting productivity and innovation negatively.

Similarly, traditional leadership has hierarchical structures that have limitations. With communication channels that are restricted and a rigid command chain, and employees may feel like they are not part of the decision making process and their contributions do not count. Their collaboration with other people is hindered, idea sharing obstructed and collective talent and wisdom ignored.

That said, it is worth mentioning that fear based command-and-control management styles geared towards only achieving results can led to a culture of fear and compliance rather than trust and empowerment. This means that they maybe micromanaged which in turn leads to lower job satisfaction rates hence underutilization of skills. The resultant effect is passive teams which cannot grow an organization.

On the other hand, iconic leadership differs from traditional leadership in its attempt to overcome these limitations by creating more inclusive and empowering conditions. Iconic leaders place emphasis on open communication among staff members as well as collaboration thereby appreciating the value of each person's opinion while seeking solutions collectively.

By employing change-oriented leadership tactics such as active listening, empathy, emotional intelligence among others; icons leaders create a strong bond between them and their subordinates. Trust is inspired in others, autonomy is encouraged in people's sphere of operation including risk taking all around safe zones for innovation fostering. This breeds improved employee satisfaction while also promoting higher levels of performance, creativity and adaptive ability whenever there is need for change.

The following chapters will discuss various aspects of iconic leadership along with practical ways to promote your own iconic leader approach. Through challenging existing norms and adopting different forms of leadership style you can be able to inspire your employees thus motivating them to attain unprecedented achievements at work.

Chapter **1**

The Visionary Prelude

Crafting Iconic Leadership: A New Era of Employee Engagement & Inspiration

In the swift, ever-changing world of modern business, powerful leadership is more important now than ever before. At a time when the dynamics of workplaces are about to change completely, the importance of iconic leadership could not have been overemphasized.

Gone are the days when the concept of 'leader' was defined within the confines of power and authority. Now it gives managers an opportunity to create such an image which attracts their subordinates, provokes their trust and loyalty. By all means, a leader ought to learn how to make use of his/her potential for becoming an iconic leader.

Cultivating an iconic leadership persona is not just about pretending or acting as if one has become one. It's about being that person with vision, courage, empathy and honesty and continually demonstrating these values in your conduct. This process of cultivation helps build up individual leaders while creating organizations that would reward and recognize these virtues.

A particular kind of leadership persona can communicate quietly a leader's dedication, commitment, and strategic view especially towards his/her team. These can impact employee morale levels significantly in addition to engagement levels and overall productivity. So how do we cultivate such a leadership persona?

The first step toward crafting an iconic leadership persona requires self-awareness - acknowledging strengths and weaknesses

Next comes aligning personal values and actions with the organization's mission and values. This way your team gets to see why you are credible enough for them to trust you as their boss. Employees get encouraged when they see that their bosses live by what they say; this entails keeping the outlined principles as well as values intact.

Authenticity also plays a vital role here. If there is effective leadership, then a leader will always be true to themselves – genuine, transparent in communication – this builds confidence among others leading to strong relationships that empower teams.

Finally, cultivating an iconic leadership persona requires resilience. Success is not always a smooth ride; it has its own share of setbacks and challenges. Resilient leaders are not exempted from such situations but have the courage to face adversity with grace and determination.

In conclusion, cultivating an iconic leadership persona requires a delicate blend of strategic vision, emotional intelligence, and authenticity. This is about setting the tone at the top - trailblazing a path of integrity, vision and resilience that others aspire to follow. Solidifying this persona is just the first step as we shall further discuss in this section. There's more than meets the eye when it comes to inspirational leadership.

Crafting a Visionary Narrative

The next stage of cultivating an iconic leadership persona is crafting a visionary narrative, one that offers direction and unites your organization under a shared purpose.

How do leaders craft such a narrative? It starts with understanding where the company currently stands and where it aims to go - its ultimate vision. In our view, this constitutes "visionary narrative" as we call it.

A good visionary narrative involves three essential elements: clearness, persistence and emotional pull.

A strong leader will not make it harder for the employees to understand the future vision of the organization, they make it easier. They do this by clearly describing what lies ahead in terms of team goals, unit goals or even organizational objectives. This can be done by explaining the vision of a company so well that any worker from any level of the firm would say exactly what it is.

Persistence: It is necessary for a leader to continuously communicate his visionary narrative. And not just at a yearly convention or when things are hard – no! Consistent communication involves frequent repetition of this vision through different means such as; emails, talks, and casual conversations ensuring its penetration throughout the organization.

Pathos: People are typically guided by emotions rather than logic alone. Therefore, an effective visionary narrative should be aimed at capturing people's hearts through appealing to their emotions. This could be achieved through expressing empathy towards employees' concerns or celebrating their achievements along the journey towards realizing the vision.

As a case in point, Martin Luther King Jr didn't say "I have a plan," instead he said "I have a dream." That was an emotional appeal about what tomorrow could look like if equality reigned today thus connecting with millions. Similarly leaders who want to craft a visionary narrative that connects with employees must tap into their emotions and sensibilities while aligning personal goals with those of their organizations.

Simon Sinek emphasizes this when he refers to his Golden Circle principle in leadership. In essence, people don't buy what you do but rather why you do it, according to him. Your 'why' is essentially your visionary narrative. When leaders effectively communicate their 'why', they inspire others to join them in their journey, making the pursuit of organizational goals much more compelling and meaningful.

In short, crafting such narratives isn't about dreaming big or setting unrealistic goals; it entails providing a clear path towards an attractive future state of affairs and linking all members of an organization, compelling them to emotionally commit to it.

A well-crafted visionary narrative will be very impactful as it will inspire trust and loyalty among employees. But its true power lies in being able to articulate a compelling vision that deeply resonates with employees thereby enhancing engagement, ambition, and creating an environment conducive for iconic leadership.

Motivation & Inspiration: Transforming Workforce Engagement

Once the right leadership image has been successfully created, and a visionary narrative has been effectively conveyed, leaders should focus on motivating and inspiring their employees.

An inspired workforce is not just engaged but highly productive, innovative oriented, committed to the organization's ideals and objectives.

So how do leaders motivate and inspire their teams? It often requires a balanced combination of different strategies along with an understanding of your workforce's unique characteristics. Let us have a closer look at some key strategies:

Intrinsic Motivation:

Often the most powerful motivation arises from within oneself. As a leader, you need to create an environment where employees are internally motivated. This entails meaningful work assignments coupled with individual recognition systems; providing for personal growth opportunities among others. When individuals feel that they are making a difference in their organization and working towards the bigger picture – they become motivated to give 110%.

Empowerment:

Empowering others is a common trait of great leaders. By doing this, it does not mean you are giving up control but rather allowing autonomy and the ability to make decisions at all levels. This is achieved when people feel that they can be trusted and valued, thus motivating them to perform their duties satisfactorily.

Transformational Leadership:

The characteristic of transformational leadership exceeds day-to-day running of operations and creates an environment for empowering followers for growth. Instead of using bonuses and promotions alone, transformational leaders inspire their teams through vision and motivation. This includes stirring passion in people that moves them beyond egoistic motives to act in the best interests of the group thereby creating an active participation and engagement within the team.

Acknowledgement & Appreciation:

Everyone likes being recognized for their hard work. A simple expression of gratitude or recognition can raise morale and improve motivation. Regular genuine appreciation promotes a positive working atmosphere that inspires employees to put more effort into their jobs.

Encouraging Creativity:

Influential leaders inspire innovative thinking and creativity among their members of staff. They know that novel ideas are needed to stay ahead in business; as such, they ask their workforce to think differently about issues affecting them – thus creating an engaged workforce.

To sum up becoming an iconic leader is not only a matter of good strategic planning or effective communication skills but also about being inspirational enough to get your subordinates self-motivated, create a conducive environment where any suggestions will be positively appreciated, recognize good work done by employees encourage creativity or go beyond normal transactional methods. Transformational leadership plays a very important role here which we shall discuss further below.

The Shift to A New Era: Emphasizing Employee Engagement

The business environment has changed signifying new relationship between heads of organizations and their subordinates. It is now moving from pure authority approach towards one based on involvement, motivation, empowerment etc. This transition ushers in a new era of leadership – from employee management to employee engagement and cultivating a growth-oriented culture. Examples showing these ideas are "New era," and "Employee engagement".

We have entered an era in which culture has changed. Leaders no longer sit back and wait for them to develop organically but they take the initiative in creating context that promotes motivation, innovation, growth, and success. Instead of focusing solely on task accomplishment or meeting targets, the focus is now on developing a highly engaged workforce that derives intrinsic satisfaction from their work.

Why is Employee Engagement Important?

Engaged employees play a vital role in organizational performance. Findings show that organizations with highly engaged employees outperform those without in many important areas such as productivity levels, improved morale amongst workers, customer satisfaction as well as retention rates. Job satisfaction does not necessarily lead to engagement since it only keeps employees happy but it entails making them feel valued in order to make them set personal goals parallel to corporate objectives.

This now begs the question; how can we build such engagement?

Instilling a Culture of Transparency:

Transparency is not just a buzzword; rather it is vital for this new age of workplace involvement. It involves leaders having clear lines of communication- sharing broad visions as well as specific goals transparently- that leads to trust and convergence towards common goals.

Fostering an Environment of Trust:

Employee engagement is profoundly impacted by trust. If workers trust their leaders – have faith in their vision, feel supported by their policies – they are more likely to be deeply involved in their work. A leader can cultivate this trust through integrity, consistency in actions and decisions, and empathy for the workforce.

Promoting a Learning Environment:

In today's fast-changing business world, continuous learning is essential. Managers should support learning continuously, provide resources for skills development, understand individual learning paths and delegate roles that will enable staff to apply new skills acquired. This does not only promote one's personal growth but also increases commitment towards work and the overall engagement of employees.

In conclusion, transitioning to a new form of leadership highlights the importance of creating a compelling work environment. It necessitates leaders who are not mere taskmasters but visionaries who inspire and mentors who guide as well as influencers who resonate with their team. Therefore, as we navigate these dynamics in our workplaces today, let us redefine our understanding of leadership so that it becomes more human-centered with every voice mattering and everyone connected to it vision-wise.

However, there are still numerous aspects that make up iconic leadership which are yet to be exhausted fully. In the next section of this paper will discuss how we can practically implement these changes within your organization so that we can come one step closer towards building an iconic leadership personality as envisaged through having outlined its relevance earlier on.

Implementation of a New Vision: Building the Foundations of Iconic Leadership

Now what is left is implementing these principles into your leadership practices after establishing how crucial it is to craft an iconic leadership persona; motivate or inspire employees; and prepare for the new era of employee engagement. This involves accepting a strategic method that interlocks values with vision then transforms them into action.

Transforming Communication:

To achieve this aim within an organizational setting, change leaders must adopt open lines of communication which are transparent enough to reach all members within their team. This entails not only communicating the bigger picture but also defining individual roles towards that vision realization. Leaders can, thus, create a situation where people understand their place by clearly stating what others expect of them and providing regular constructive feedbacks to make sure everything is on track and aligned properly.

Adopting Participative Decision-Making:

Generally, organizations that involve employees in decision-making tend to perform better in today's ever-changing business environment. An engaged workforce is more likely to result when employees believe that their thoughts matter. Therefore, leaders aspiring to become iconic should encourage conversations, appreciate multiple viewpoints and promote participative decision-making - acknowledging the collective intelligence existing within their teams.

Nurturing Innovation:

An inspirational leader creates an environment where innovation thrives. Encouraging creativity is no longer about brainstorming or suggestion boxes; it is about building a culture in which any employee feels confident enough to expose innovative ideas without fear of being ridiculed or rejected. Leaders should celebrate novel thinking at all levels – appreciating that every contribution gets the organization closer to its ultimate purpose.

Promoting Continuous Learning:

To keep pace with the changing market trends, and customer demands, continuous learning should be a priority for businesses. It is important for the leaders to create an environment where constant education is welcomed and rewarded. This may involve such things as investing in professional development programs, providing access to online courses, organizing in-house training sessions – which help employees satisfy their personal aspirations and facilitate competitive advantage for the organization.

Embracing Emotional Intelligence:

Leadership in the 21st century: The importance of emotional intelligence cannot be overstressed. Building trust, enhancing communication and fostering meaningful relationships by understanding and managing one's emotions as well as those of team members are significant attributes of iconic leadership.

Ultimately implementing a new vision within your organization involves more than just communicating goals and setting performance indicators. It requires empowering leadership that encourages open dialogue, drives innovation, promotes continuous learning and is heavily based on emotional intelligence. Remember that a journey of one thousand miles begins with a single step – so why not start incorporating these strategies into your leadership style today?

Chapter 2

Authenticity Unleashed

Authenticity Unleashed: Authentic Leadership's Power in Building Trust & Credibility

Leadership, in its most fundamental essence, isn't merely about delegating tasks or monitoring performance. It's intrinsically tied to the capacity to inspire, motivate, and connect with people on a deeper level. In this context, the importance of authenticity cannot be overstated. Indeed, as we move forward into an era where values and trust are becoming increasingly central to effective leadership, the concept of 'Authentic Leadership' plays a pivotal role.

So, what does Authentic Leadership mean? Simply put, it refers to being genuine and true to oneself in a leadership role. It is the integrity of character that compels others to follow not out of obligation but due to genuine respect and admiration. An authentic leader walks the talk, stays consistent in their values, and doesn't shy away from showing vulnerability. They are neither afraid of exposing their weaknesses nor do they feel the need to feign perfection.

However, this raises a compelling question: why is Authentic Leadership essential? To respond, let's delve into the rapidly evolving landscape of today's corporate world. It's one where employees value transparency and honesty perhaps more than anything else. They yearn for leaders who are both relatable and inspiring; those who lead by example while maintaining their unique individuality and humanity.

In such a dynamic space, an authentic leader can indeed be a game-changer. By promoting an environment grounded in trust and openness, they can foster meaningful relationships with employees. This not only improves morale but also stimulates productivity and fosters mutual growth.

Moreover, authentic leadership is essential because it encourages accountability, promotes inclusivity, and empowers individuals within the organization. An authentic leader does not merely 'rule over' employees; instead, they inspire them to evolve into better versions of themselves.

By consistently demonstrating credibility and ethical behaviour, an authentic leader can create a powerful ripple effect within the organization. This can instill a culture of trust, inspire authenticity in others, and ultimately transform the very fabric of the organization.

From start-ups grappling to find their footings, through to multinational corporations striving to navigate unprecedented challenges, authentic leadership holds the potential to steer organizations towards success. But harnessing this approach is not just about flipping a switch. It requires an in-depth understanding of its core characteristics and a commitment to live them out in practice. As we dive deeper into this topic, we shall look closer at these characteristics and how they shape a truly authentic leader.

In essence, Authentic Leadership is not just a strategy or a model; it's a way of life. As we peel back the layers of this concept, we'll discover why it's vital for today's leaders and how they can unleash their authenticity to build trust, credibility and ultimately impact their organizations positively.

As we proceed deeper into our exploration of Authentic Leadership, it becomes necessary to lay out the key defining characteristics and traits that form its DNA. These foundational elements are the crucial differentiators that set authentic leaders apart and give authenticity its transformative power in leadership.

Self-Awareness

A core trait of an authentic leader is self-awareness. They have a profound understanding of their strengths, weaknesses, values, emotions, and the effect they have on others. This awareness allows them to align their actions with their inner values consistently, modelling a behaviour that nurtures trust within teams.

Genuine Communication

Authentic leaders prioritize transparent and open communication. They take the initiative to express their thoughts clearly and listen attentively to others' perspectives. Their genuine interaction fosters a culture of openness, thereby enhancing mutual respect and understanding.

Consistency in Values

An authentic leader remains steadfast in their values under all circumstances. Through consistent action and decision-making guided by ethics and integrity, they create a trustworthy environment where individuals feel motivated to give their best.

Navigating Vulnerability

Rather than perceiving vulnerability as weakness, authentic leaders embrace it as a channel for deepening connections with employees. It's about acknowledging mistakes, learning from them, and moving forward with grace. This human approach enhances credibility as employees view their leader as relatable rather than unapproachable.

Pursuing Purpose beyond Profit

An unwavering characteristic of authentic leadership is the pursuit of purpose beyond profit. Leaders who align their work with a larger mission or social cause inspire employees to do the same. This sense of higher purpose instills motivation, commitment, and dedication among team members towards shared objectives.

In essence, these traits serve as the building blocks in shaping an authentic leadership style. But it's also crucial to understand that becoming an authentic leader is not an overnight achievement. It demands constant self-reflection, openness to feedback, and a commitment to personal growth.

Beyond its intrinsic benefits, Authentic Leadership brings tangible results in fostering a healthier organisational climate. And while embodying these traits requires continuous effort and alignment, the reward lies in establishing trustful and resilient teams driven by values and common goals.

The transformative power of authenticity in leadership is undeniably effective when applied with commitment and consistency. The result is leaders who are not only respected for their role but admired for their character. They lead by example, setting a precedent of transparency, integrity, empathy, and determination that permeates throughout the organisation.

The path to authentic leadership is both personal and profound; it's about leading with your true self. As we continue this exploration into Authentic Leadership's power in Building Trust

& Credibility, we'll delve deeper into how authenticity can establish trust dynamics within teams, enhancing overall performance and productivity.

Building Trust through Authentic Leadership

A significant pillar of authentic leadership is the ability to foster trust within an organization. An environment shadowed by doubt and suspicion is hardly conducive to productive work, innovation, or sustained growth. Conversely, when team members are assured of their leader's credibility and consistency, they feel empowered and motivated to perform to their full potential.

In establishing trust dynamics within an organization, authentic leaders utilize several strategies. For starters, they consistently manifest integrity in all interactions - whether it's a high-stake client negotiation or a casual conversation with a colleague. By aligning actions with stated values and maintaining transparency, these leaders tangibly demonstrate that they can be trusted.

Authentic leaders also foster trust by taking a stakeholder-oriented approach. They appreciate the unique value every team member brings and engage them with respect and dignity. Additionally, such leaders understand the importance of maintaining open lines of communication. This involves not only conveying decisions and policies effectively but also being receptive to feedback and suggestions from employees.

Examples of Trust-Building in Authentic Leadership

To illustrate this concept further, consider few real-life examples involving widely recognized authentic leaders.

Take Howard Schultz, the former CEO of Starbucks. He was known for his dedication towards maintaining an open dialogue with his employees—referred to as 'partners' within the company. He would frequently visit Starbucks stores across the globe, meeting partners at all levels and genuinely listening to their thoughts and concerns. This open communication strategy built significant trust within the company, fueling its phenomenal growth over the years.

Another noteworthy example is Paul Polman, the ex-CEO of Unilever. He established an ambitious vision for the company - doubling its size while reducing its environmental footprint. But rather than imposing this challenging goal top-down, he spent considerable effort engaging with employees at all levels, articulating the vision and inspiring them to partake in its realization. This stakeholder-oriented approach cultivated a strong sense of trust within the organization, propelling it towards significant success.

These examples reveal that establishing trust isn't about grand gestures or mere words; it's primarily about demonstrating consistency and respect within everyday actions. It involves embracing transparency, promoting open dialogue, appreciating diversity, and displaying a steadfast commitment to shared values.

The Ripple Effect of Trust in an Organization

When leaders are able to successfully embed these principles within their leadership style, they create an atmosphere of trust within the organization—a culture where employees feel safe expressing ideas, sharing concerns or making suggestions. This confidence has numerous benefits including increased job satisfaction, higher rates of productivity and improved overall team performance.

In conclusion, building trust is not just an ancillary benefit of authentic leadership—it's one of its major goals. By developing an environment characterized by openness, integrity and mutual respect, authentic leaders enhance their credibility while driving the organization towards greater heights.

Fostering this culture requires patience and determination—after all, trust is earned over time. However, by maintaining unwavering commitment towards this objective amidst daily challenges and pressures, leaders can ultimately achieve a profound transformation in the way their teams operate and perform.

Authentic Leadership - A Path to Credibility

In the sphere of leadership, credibility isn't conferred through title or position. Instead, it is earned through consistent authenticity, trustworthy actions, and a steadfast adherence to one's values. The inextricable link between authentic leadership and organizational credibility has been underscored by countless studies and is evident in the success narratives of numerous organizations.

Credibility matters for an organization because it directly influences employees' motivation levels, their commitment to the organization, and their overall performance. When team members perceive leaders as credible, they are more likely to trust decisions made at the top level, engage constructively in problem-solving discussions, and express greater job satisfaction. Consequently, fostering credibility is not just a nice-to-have but also a must-have element in any leadership approach.

At the heart of achieving such credibility lies the concept of 'authentic leadership.' Authentic leaders build credibility by being transparent with their intentions, consistent in their actions, reliable in delivering on their promises, and receptive towards others' opinions. They engage openly with team members and stakeholders, demonstrating a genuine interest in understanding their perspectives and addressing their questions or concerns.

The Impact of Authenticity on Credibility

An authentic leader establishes credibility by demonstrating consistency between words and actions. For example, if a leader talks about promoting a culture of innovation but doesn't provide sufficient resources or flexibility for team members to experiment with new ideas, then that leader's credibility will inevitably get impacted negatively. On the other hand, when words align seamlessly with action, such consistency reinforces the faith of team members in their leader's competence and integrity.

Moreover, authenticity enhances credibility by fostering greater connection and empathy between leaders and team members. By displaying vulnerability at appropriate moments—like admitting mistakes or discussing challenges—leaders show that they are human, just like everyone else. This candidness renders leaders more relatable and approachable, strengthening the bonds of trust within teams and boosting their overall credibility.

Research Studies Linking Authentic Leadership to Credibility

The correlation between authentic leadership and credibility is not merely speculative but has been validated by several research studies. For instance, a study published in the Journal of

Business Ethics found that authentic leadership boosts employees' psychological capital and job performance while reducing cynicism about organizational change.

In another study published in the Leadership Quarterly journal, researchers discovered that teams led by authentic leaders exhibited higher levels of trust and satisfaction along with lower turnover rates. The same study revealed how authentic leadership leads to positive team identification and enhanced team efficacy, eventually culminating in improved organizational performance.

These findings underscore the profound impact of authentic leadership in shaping organizational culture, guiding employee behaviors, and driving business outcomes. They also reiterate the importance of adhering to an authentic leadership style for enhancing credibility within organizations.

Establishing robust credibility through authentic leadership is undeniably challenging. It necessitates courage, self-awareness, continual learning, and above all else—authenticity. However, leaders who bravely embrace this path will cultivate invaluable assets: organizational trust and credibility - pillars that can hold strong even amidst turbulence or uncertainty.

In conclusion, it's evident that authenticity doesn't just contribute to effective leadership—it forms its bedrock. By consistently demonstrating authenticity in words and actions, leaders can build an environment where trust thrives, augmented by high credibility levels—resulting in a happy workforce as well as phenomenal organizational success!

A Practical Guide: Vulnerability and Navigating Interactions at a Deeper Level

The essence of authentic leadership is influenced significantly by vulnerability. By recognizing and navigating the delicate balance of vulnerability in leadership, managers can foster deeper connections with their employees. Here, we offer insights into how embracing vulnerability can serve to strengthen interpersonal relationships within teams while maintaining the crucial respect and trust integral to effective leadership.

Understanding the role of Vulnerability in Leadership

Traditionally, expressions of vulnerability have been considered counterproductive in the world of leadership, often seen as evidence of weakness that could be exploited. However, modern discussions on authentic leadership are challenging this notion. True strength lies not in being impervious but rather in confronting vulnerability and employing it as a tool for connection.

Embracing vulnerability involves leaders acknowledging their shortcomings or errors openly. This transparency lends authenticity to their positions, making them more relatable to their employees who likely experience similar insecurities themselves.

Striking the Balance - Navigating Vulnerability Authentically

Maintaining an optimal balance when navigating vulnerability is key to fostering authentic connections without compromising the leadership role's integrity. Leaders should practice openness about their mistakes or doubts; however, they must also demonstrate resilience and a commitment to personal growth. This combination conveys that while they too are fallible human beings, they possess the resolve necessary for driving progress even when faced with setbacks.

Vulnerability - A Channel for Deeper Connections

Leaders who effectively navigate vulnerability create an environment where honesty is valued over concealing imperfections. This encourages employees to voice their thoughts without fear of being judged or penalized for admitting errors or expressing doubts.

This culture promotes deeper connections as individuals feel seen, heard and understood – factors that contribute significantly to their sense of belonging and overall engagement with the organization.

Tips for Leaders: Navigating Vulnerability

1. **Self-awareness:** Be aware of personal strengths, weaknesses, and emotions. Self-awareness enables leaders to initiate open conversations about their areas of improvement without feeling threatened or defensive.
2. **Receptiveness:** Encourage feedback and cultivate an atmosphere where constructive criticism is seen as a tool for growth rather than an attack on competence.
3. **Courageous Conversations:** Be brave in addressing difficult topics or admitting mistakes. It sends a strong message that owning up to one's faults is part of the process and not a sign of weakness.
4. **Balancing Act:** While expressing vulnerabilities, ensure not to overdo it. Excessive sharing may lead to questionable professional boundaries; thus, maintain balance by sharing experiences relevant to work life instead of delving too deep into personal struggles.
5. Acknowledging imperfections can be daunting yet powerful in shaping authentic leadership within organizations. By navigating vulnerability effectively, leaders can connect meaningfully with employees, building trust, mutual respect, and credibility necessary for any thriving workforce.

The Bottom Line

In essence, navigating vulnerability paves the way for deeper connections between leaders and employees. It establishes trust and provides valuable lessons about growth and resilience. While vulnerability may appear paradoxical to traditional leadership concepts, it ultimately fortifies the foundation of authenticity providing a leadership style resonating deeply with today's workforce.

Examples of Authentic Leadership in Action

To better understand how authentic leadership can be applied in different contexts, let's explore a few real-life examples:

Steve Jobs: A Visionary Innovator

Steve Jobs, the co-founder of Apple Inc., is often cited as an example of an authentic leader. He had a clear vision for the future of technology and was passionate about creating innovative products that would revolutionize the industry. Jobs was known for his intense focus, attention to detail, and commitment to excellence. He was not afraid to take risks and challenge conventional wisdom, often pushing his team to their limits. Despite his demanding nature, Jobs inspired his followers with his unwavering belief in their abilities and the potential of their work.

Oprah Winfrey: Empowering Others

Oprah Winfrey, media mogul and philanthropist, is a prime example of an authentic leader who uses her platform to empower others. Through her talk show, books, and philanthropic efforts, Winfrey has inspired millions of people around the world to live their best lives. She has been open about her own struggles and experiences, using her authenticity to connect with her audience on a deep level. Winfrey's empathy, compassion, and commitment to social justice have made her a respected and influential figure.

Nelson Mandela: Leading with Forgiveness

Nelson Mandela, the late South African president and anti-apartheid activist, is widely regarded as an authentic leader who led with forgiveness and reconciliation. Despite spending 27 years in prison, Mandela emerged with a deep sense of compassion and a commitment to building a united and inclusive nation. His ability to forgive his oppressors and work towards a peaceful transition to democracy inspired people around the world. Mandela's authenticity, humility, and unwavering belief in the power of forgiveness made him a symbol of hope and reconciliation.

Pros and Cons of Authentic Leadership

While authentic leadership has many benefits, it is important to recognize that it may not be suitable for every situation. Let's explore some of the pros and cons of the authentic leadership approach:

Pros:

- **Trust and engagement:** Authentic leaders inspire trust and create a sense of psychological safety, leading to higher levels of employee engagement and commitment.

- **Positive ethical climate:** Authentic leaders prioritize ethical behavior and set high ethical standards for themselves and their followers, fostering a positive ethical climate within the organization.

- **Improved decision-making:** Authentic leaders seek diverse perspectives and consider different viewpoints, leading to more informed and balanced decision-making processes.

- Increased job satisfaction: Authentic leaders create a supportive and inclusive work environment, leading to higher levels of job satisfaction and well-being among employees.

Cons:

- **Inappropriate in high-risk situations:** The authentic leadership style may not be suitable in high-risk or emergency situations where quick and decisive action is required.

- **Potential for diminished innovation:** The moral superiority often associated with authentic leaders may inadvertently discourage innovative thinking and suggestions from followers.

- **Time-consuming:** Developing and embodying an authentic leadership style requires self-reflection, introspection, and continuous personal growth, which can be time-consuming for leaders.

Developing Authentic Leadership Skills

Developing authentic leadership skills requires a combination of self-reflection, learning, and practice. Here are some strategies and exercises that can help leaders enhance their authenticity:

Self-reflection and introspection

Take the time to reflect on your values, beliefs, strengths, and weaknesses. Understand what drives you and what is important to you. Regularly assess your actions and behaviors to ensure they align with your authentic self.

Seek feedback

Ask for feedback from your followers, peers, and mentors. Actively listen to their perspectives and be open to constructive criticism. Use the feedback to identify areas for growth and improvement.

Share your stories

Share personal stories and experiences with your followers. Be vulnerable and authentic in your storytelling, as this will help build trust and connection. Share stories of challenges, failures, and successes to inspire and motivate others.

Practice empathy

Develop your empathy skills by putting yourself in others' shoes and seeking to understand their perspectives and emotions. Show genuine care and concern for your followers, and consider their needs and aspirations when making decisions.

Align actions with values

Ensure that your actions and behaviors are consistent with your core values and ethical standards. Make decisions that reflect your beliefs and principles, even in challenging situations.

Lifelong learning

Commit to continuous learning and personal growth. Stay curious, seek new knowledge and skills, and be open to different perspectives. Embrace feedback as an opportunity for growth.

Build strong relationships

Invest time and effort in building strong relationships with your followers. Foster open and honest communication, and create a supportive and inclusive work environment where everyone feels valued and respected.

Authentic leadership is a powerful and effective leadership style that inspires trust, fosters engagement, and promotes positive change. By embodying their true selves, authentic leaders create a sense of authenticity and transparency that resonates with their followers. Developing authentic leadership skills requires self-reflection, learning, and practice, but the benefits are well worth the effort. As you embark on your own journey towards authentic leadership, remember the words of Mahatma Gandhi: *"Be the change that you wish to see in the world."*

Let your authenticity be the catalyst for positive transformation, both in yourself and in those you lead.

Chapter **3**

Crafting an Iconic Brand

Merging Personal, Leadership & Branding Strategies for Success

Laying the Foundation: The Importance of Crafting a Personal Brand

In today's highly competitive marketplace, crafting a personal brand has never been more crucial. It serves as your business card, embodying your unique value proposition and setting you apart from the competition. Your personal brand is not simply your work persona but a reflection of your values, passions, skills, and experiences that collectively form the perception people have about you.

Keywords such as *"personal brand"* and *"crafting a brand"* are often associated with successful managers and leaders who have managed to make their mark in their respective fields due to effective personal branding. It helps shape your professional identity, enhances your reputation, attracts opportunities, and paves the way for long-term success.

One vital aspect of creating an impactful personal brand is aligning it with your organization's core values. A disconnect between the two can damage both your personal reputation and the company's overall image. Therefore, understanding and embodying your organization's *"core values in brand building"* ensures you are working towards the same mission and vision, resulting in stronger engagement with stakeholders and clients.

This alignment doesn't just enhance organizational coherence; it also supports the development of an *"enduring brand,"* which stands the test of time and remains relevant despite changing market conditions. An enduring brand resonates with its target audience on an emotional level, outlives trends, and is flexible enough to adapt to change while maintaining its core essence.

To craft an impactful and enduring personal brand, it's important to start with a solid foundation built upon introspection. Reflect on what you value most, what drives you, and how you wish others to perceive you. Combine these insights with introspection on your skills, unique qualities, and experiences to form a comprehensive picture of your personal brand.

Remember, authenticity is key when crafting your personal brand because it's the true you that people connect with. Authenticity encourages trust, inspires loyalty, and allows you to establish meaningful relationships with colleagues, clients, and industry peers. It also sets the stage for your leadership style and guides every decision and action, making a foundation for an iconic brand.

Crafting a personal brand is a strategic process that requires continuous effort, self-awareness, and consistency. However, the resulting clarity of focus, differentiation in the marketplace, and connection with your audience make it a worthwhile investment.

Leading by Distinction: Building Unique Iconic Leadership Styles

Once the foundation of your personal brand is firmly laid, it is time to turn towards developing a unique leadership style that resonates with and reinforces this distinct identity. A well-defined *"leadership style"* aligns closely with your personal brand and helps carve out your signature path in your professional journey.

In contrast to popular belief, leadership is not a one-size-fits-all concept. There are different styles of leadership, each effective given its appropriate context. These variations represent *"unique elements in leadership"*, reflecting a leader's personality traits, attitudes, values, and behaviours.

Distinguishing yourself as an exemplary leader means identifying and implementing the leadership style that best aligns with you as an individual and a professional. Whether transformational or transactional, democratic or laissez-faire, each leadership style presents its unique benefits.

A real leader stands out because of his or her ability to adapt their style depending on the team's needs and the organization's goals. This flexibility allows leaders to be effective across various scenarios and work environments. For instance, the democrat might encourage participative decision-making during brainstorming sessions while adopting a more directive approach when meeting tight deadlines.

Your own distinctive style can often be considered an *"extraordinary leadership."* Extraordinary leaders are not defined by holding a high-ranking position or having years of experience but by their impactful actions, influential decisions, vision-driven strategies, and empathetic communication. They lead from their hearts and minds together, inspiring others through their passion for their work.

In developing your unique leadership style, there are certain factors to consider. Firstly, self-awareness is vital in understanding your strengths and weaknesses. Managers can leverage their strengths while working on areas of improvement.

Additionally, an exceptional leader always seeks feedback from his or her team members. This openness to input not only encourages a transparent culture within the organization but also provides valuable insights for the leader's personal and professional growth.

Lastly, mastering effective communication is instrumental in establishing a unique leadership style. It allows managers to articulate their vision clearly, ensuring that everyone is on the same page, decreasing confusion and increasing productivity.

In conclusion, a distinct leadership style aligned with your personal brand will significantly add to your effectiveness as a leader. It showcases your authenticity, increases emotional connections with your followers, and helps you stand out in today's competitive marketplace. So take time to cultivate your unique leadership style – it's well worth the effort.

Brand-Builder Actions: Aligning Communication Strategies and Actions towards Branding Success

In crafting a personal brand and defining your unique leadership style, it's crucial to understand that these are not static concepts but rather, evolving entities. Your actions and communication methods play a significant role in moulding your brand and impacting how others perceive you as a leader. This section focuses on aligning *"communication strategies"* and *"actions for brand building"* to ensure a successful branding trajectory.

Effective communication is instrumental in the establishment of a strong personal brand. It helps articulate your vision, values, and style effectively. A well-defined *"communication strategy"* not only delivers your message accurately but also builds trust among stakeholders and audiences. When you communicate transparently and regularly, people get to know who you are, what you stand for, and what to expect from you.

Your *"actions for brand building"* define your credibility. Every decision you make or step you take contributes to consolidating or undermining your brand identity. Therefore, aligning actions with stated values is critical. Consistency in action displays integrity and reliability – both key attributes for successful leadership.

Besides being consistent, your actions should display value addition as well. As a leader, every move should add value to the team or organization. Be it coaching employees, improving processes, driving innovation, or encouraging collaboration; all these reflect positively on your personal brand.

Fostering positivity through impactful actions can also help inspire *"trust and brand consistency."* When leaders consistently follow their words with action, followers find them reliable. They know they can depend on such leaders in any situation, which fosters trustworthiness.

Actions also speak volumes when it comes to conflict resolution. Leaders who handle conflicts assertively and diplomatically stand out. They use such situations as opportunities for learning and growth, reinforcing their brand's strength.

Your communication strategy and actions should also reinforce each other. Coherent messages get strengthened when backed by consistent actions. Contrarily, inconsistent actions can confuse stakeholders, leading to diluted brand value.

How you communicate your vision and execute actions significantly impacts your personal branding. Therefore, make sure that every communication aligns seamlessly with your personal brand narrative, and every action reflects the values you stand for. As you consistently align your communication strategies and brand-building actions, you strengthen your leadership image – paving the way for a more influential and impactful personal brand.

Safeguarding your Identity: Maintaining a Consistent Brand Identity over Time

Once you've crafted a compelling personal brand and developed an aligned leadership style, another equally crucial task awaits—maintaining brand consistency. This is not a one-off task but rather requires ongoing commitment to uphold the characteristics that define your personal brand.

In today's digital age where multi-faceted platforms are available, managing an *"consistent brand identity"* can be challenging. Despite this, it is essential to ensure that each point of contact with your target audience—be it through social media posts, press releases, email newsletters, or face-to-face interactions—exhibits your unique brand persona consistently.

Firms often maintain multiple brands under the same umbrella—a *"multi-brand portfolio."* Here too, leaders should ensure consistency while allowing each brand its unique flavor. The similar underlying values help reinforce the parent brand across all sub-brands. Just like Unilever successfully manages Dove or Axe with their distinct identities, yet being part of the broader Unilever ethos.

In ensuring consistency in your personal brand identity, understand that evolution is inevitable and necessary. As you grow professionally and personally, some aspects of your brand will also evolve. The key lies in ensuring that these changes do not disrupt the core essence of your personal brand.

An effective method for maintaining a consistent message across platforms is embracing *"integrated marketing communication."* This approach helps synergize all promotional methods used by a leader or firm ensuring they work together towards a common objective and deliver a unified message. It also helps boost the effectiveness of each marketing tool by reinforcing their collective impact.

A powerful platform for maintaining consistent branding in today's era is social media. The ubiquitous presence of social media has made *"social media branding"* an integral part of personal brand management. Leaders can utilize platforms like LinkedIn, Twitter, or Instagram to share insights, express opinions, inspire followers and communicate their brand's message effectively.

However, it's essential to approach social media with caution as inconsistencies here are most visible and can hurt your personal brand identity. An overarching strategy that outlines the type of content to be shared, frequency of updates and tonality can help maintain consistency across different channels.

Maintaining a consistent brand identity over time requires deliberate planning and execution. While it isn't easy, it's certainly worthwhile. A strong, consistent identity forms the backbone of any successful brand—personal or corporate—and lays the foundation for trust, loyalty, and long-term success.

The Psychology behind Branding & Diversity Inclusion in Organizations

While creating and maintaining a brand, many managers overlook the deep-seated psychological aspects that influence how their brand is perceived. This includes aspects like *"color psychology in branding"* as well as the diversity, equity, and inclusion practices within the organization.

Color plays a significant role in perception. As part of *"color psychology in branding,"* it's essential to understand that different colors invoke diverse emotions. For example, red can symbolize excitement or passion, while blue often represents trust and stability. Selecting the right colors for your personal brand can influence people's perceptions of you.

Apart from color, other visual elements such as logos, symbols, or typography also play a crucial role in communicating your brand identity effectively. A well-designed logo, for instance, can make a lasting impression and drive recognition for your personal brand. Understanding these subtle but powerful elements can help create an emotionally appeasing and impactful personal brand.

As our understanding of organizational dynamics evolves, an important factor that emerges is the impact of *"diversity, equity, and inclusion in organizations."* Incorporating diversity not only broadens perspectives within an organization but also makes a strong statement about the leader's commitment to inclusivity - a trait increasingly valued in contemporary work environments.

Fostering an inclusive culture demonstrates empathy and respect for individual differences - qualities that resonate positively with both internal teams and external stakeholders. An emphasis on building diverse teams reflects a forward-thinking mindset that values gaining varied insights by leveraging different ethnicities, genders, age groups, experiences and skill sets.

Beyond just rhetoric or superficial measures, true inclusion requires implementing policies that guarantee equity in opportunities, allowing everyone to participate and contribute meaningfully. Authenticity in these practices strengthens your personal brand as a dynamic and empathetic leader.

Aspects of an inclusive leadership style such as active listening, embracing different perspectives, fostering an open culture where everyone feels valued for their contributions, can be powerful tools for reinforcing the manager's brand identity.

Including *"diversity, equity, and inclusion in organizations"* as part of your personal brand strategy might also involve championing for change, being an advocate for those unheard or underrepresented. This shows commitment beyond just professional growth - it signifies social responsibility that propagates positive societal impact.

To sum up, understanding the psychology behind branding and being committed to diversity and inclusion is indispensable for crafting a robust and iconic personal brand. It is a holistic approach that requires leaders to delve deeper into aspects that influence perception while simultaneously fostering an inclusive environment within their teams and organizations.

Chapter 4

Connecting Through Storytelling in Business: Unleashing the Power of Narrative

In today's competitive and noisy market, standing out from the crowd is crucial for entrepreneurs, business owners, and leaders. One powerful tool that can help you distinguish yourself and connect with your audience on a deeper level is storytelling. Stories have the ability to captivate attention, evoke emotions, and inspire action. In this section, we will explore the art of storytelling in business, its benefits, and strategies to master it effectively.

What is Storytelling and Why Does it Matter?

At its core, storytelling is the art of crafting narratives that capture the essence of your brand and resonate with your audience. It goes beyond the features and benefits of your product or service, delving into the emotional and psychological aspects of decision-making. Storytelling has been an integral part of human culture for centuries, transcending language, culture, and religion. It is a universal communication tool that connects us all.

The Benefits of Storytelling in Business

Building Trust and Rapport with Your Audience

In the world of business, people buy from those they trust and like. Storytelling allows you to showcase your personality, values, and authenticity, establishing a bond with your audience. By sharing stories that reflect your brand's identity, you create a sense of trust, making customers more inclined to choose your products or services.

Differentiating Your Brand from Competitors

In a crowded marketplace, it's essential to differentiate your brand from competitors. Storytelling provides a unique opportunity to highlight what sets you apart. By telling your story in a compelling and authentic way, you can showcase your unique selling proposition and attract customers who resonate with your narrative.

Creating Memorable and Shareable Content

In a world inundated with information, capturing attention is key. Stories have the power to cut through the noise and make an impact. By incorporating storytelling into your content strategy, you can create memorable and shareable content that stands out in the minds of your audience. Whether through blog posts, videos, or social media campaigns, storytelling helps your message stick and encourages others to spread the word.

Increasing Engagement and Loyalty

Emotional connection plays a vital role in customer engagement and loyalty. Stories have the ability to evoke emotions, creating a lasting impression on your audience. By crafting narratives that resonate with their desires, fears, and aspirations, you can deepen their connection to your brand. This emotional spark drives engagement, retention, and loyalty, fostering long-term relationships with your customers.

Driving Sales and Conversions

Stories have the power to influence decision-making by appealing to emotions. People often make choices based on how they feel, and then justify them with logic. By leveraging storytelling techniques, you can tap into your audience's emotions, motivate them to take action, and overcome objections or fears. Stories create a sense of urgency, driving sales and conversions.

Mastering the Art of Storytelling for Your Business

Now that we understand the importance of storytelling in business, let's delve into strategies to master this art and effectively connect with your audience.

Know Your Audience and Their Pain Points

To craft compelling stories, you must first understand your audience. Conduct thorough research to identify their needs, wants, challenges, and aspirations. By profiling your ideal customers, you can tailor your narratives to resonate with their experiences, making your stories relatable and impactful.

Define Your Core Message and Value Proposition

Clarify the main message you want to convey through your stories and define your value proposition. What problem does your brand solve, and how does it benefit your audience? Craft a concise and compelling statement that encapsulates your brand's mission and the unique value it offers.

Choose the Right Format and Channel for Your Story

Different stories require different formats and channels. Consider where your target audience spends their time online and what types of content they prefer. Whether it's through blog articles, videos, podcasts, or social media posts, choose the medium that best suits your story and aligns with your audience's preferences.

Use the Classic Storytelling Structure

A well-crafted story follows a classic structure that engages the audience from start to finish. Begin by introducing your characters, including your brand and your audience. Set the stage by presenting the situation or problem your audience faces, followed by the obstacles or challenges they encounter. Finally, reveal how your brand's solution or value proposition resolves the conflict and helps your audience achieve their desired outcome.

Incorporate Sensory Details and Emotions

To make your stories come alive, incorporate vivid sensory details that appeal to your audience's imagination. Engage their senses of sight, sound, smell, taste, and touch to create a captivating experience. Additionally, tap into their emotions by highlighting the emotional journey of your characters and evoking feelings that resonate with your audience's desires and aspirations.

Examples of Effective Storytelling in Business

Let's explore some real-world examples of businesses that have successfully leveraged storytelling to connect with their audience and achieve remarkable results.

Apple: Inspiring Innovation and Creativity

Apple is renowned for its compelling storytelling, emphasizing innovation, creativity, and the pursuit of excellence. Their iconic "Think Different" campaign celebrated individuals who challenged the status quo and changed the world. Through their stories, Apple created an emotional connection with their audience, inspiring them to embrace their own creativity and think differently.

Nike: Empowering Athletes and Overcoming Challenges

Nike's storytelling revolves around empowering athletes and overcoming challenges. Their iconic "Just Do It" campaign features stories of athletes who faced adversity and triumphed through determination and perseverance. These narratives resonate with their audience, inspiring them to push beyond their limits and achieve greatness.

Elon Musk: Pioneering the Future of Innovation

Elon Musk, the visionary founder of SpaceX and Tesla, has mastered the art of storytelling. Through his interviews and presentations, he shares his vision of a sustainable future and the importance of pushing boundaries. By weaving together his personal journey and the potential impact of his ventures, Musk captivates his audience, inspiring them to believe in the power of innovation and change.

Martin Luther King Jr.: Inspiring Social Change

Martin Luther King Jr.'s "I Have a Dream" speech is a testament to the power of storytelling in inspiring social change. Through his words, he painted a vivid picture of a future where racial equality prevailed. By combining powerful storytelling techniques with a compelling message, King galvanized a movement and left a lasting impact on generations to come.

In today's competitive business landscape, storytelling has emerged as a powerful tool to connect with your audience, differentiate your brand, and drive meaningful engagement. By harnessing the emotional and persuasive power of narratives, you can build trust, create memorable experiences, and drive action. Remember to know your audience, define your core message, choose the right format, use a classic storytelling structure, and incorporate sensory details and emotions into your narratives. Join the ranks of successful brands and leaders who have harnessed the power of storytelling to leave a lasting impact on their audience and drive business success.

Chapter 5

Mastering Cultural Resonance: Fostering Pride and Belonging in Organizational Shifts

Organizational Culture and Cultural Resonance

In the contemporary professional landscape, organizational culture holds a position of supreme importance. This term often refers to the shared values, beliefs, and behaviors that dictate how a team interacts within an organization. It shapes your team's understanding of 'how things are done around here.' An effective organizational culture promotes efficiency, growth, and satisfaction among employees and stakeholders alike.

However, as businesses evolve, so must their cultures. The cultural shift is a natural and necessary process that occurs when organizations adapt to new market conditions, technologies, or objectives. This challenging period of transition requires careful management to ensure that it does not disrupt the harmony and productivity in a workplace.

This is where the concept of cultural resonance comes into play. Cultural resonance can be defined as the degree to which a culture's values and practices resonate with its members. It means that the elements of your organizational culture are not just accepted but deeply shared and celebrated among your employees. When cultural resonance is high, employees feel a deep sense of belonging, identify personally with their roles, and take pride in their contributions to the organization. They're more engaged, committed, productive, and likely to stay with the organization long term.

The principle of cultural resonance applies not only within an organization but also in its external face. It is about ensuring that your company's public actions reflect its inner values - this includes everything from marketing campaigns to customer service, from product delivery to corporate social responsibility efforts.

The key to achieving cultural resonance lies in its strategic cultivation. In other words, you need to assess your current organizational culture, pinpoint what needs changing, then strategically align those changes with the existing culture so they're accepted and incorporated organically. This process is not always easy, but it's crucial to the long-term health and success of a business.

In the forthcoming sections, we will delve deeper into the dynamics of a manager's iconic image, assessing and influencing organizational culture, effective strategies for cultural shift, fostering a sense of belonging and pride among employees, thereby achieving a complete cultural resonance in organizations. These insights are derived from comprehensive research, expert opinions, and successful case studies.

The Importance of a Manager's Iconic Image in Cultivating Cultural Shifts

A crucial element behind successful cultural shifts within an organization is the role played by a **manager's iconic image**. A manager is not merely an administrative figure but also a source of inspiration and leadership for their team members. The way they conduct themselves, especially in times of change, significantly influences how employees perceive and respond to new cultural paradigms within the organization.

An iconic manager is one who establishes a strong identity that aligns with the organization's values and visions. This identity can create an emotional connection between employees and the organization itself—inspiring loyalty, commitment, and motivation to contribute to the overall success of the enterprise.

The potency of a manager's iconic image lies in its ability to symbolize certain ideals or principles that the organization wishes to propagate. Employees tend to look up to their managers as role models and mentors. Therefore, it becomes essential that managers embody the changes they wish their teams to adopt. Their behavior mirrors the expectations from the team members during a cultural shift.

Having said this, creating an influential managerial image does not happen overnight. It involves consistent effort towards demonstrating professional efficacy coupled with personal charisma. Managers need to consistently display qualities like integrity, transparency, and empathy in their actions to build trust among their subordinates.

In terms of fostering cultural resonance, managers play an instrumental role through their iconic images. By exemplifying desired behaviors or attitudes associated with a cultural shift, they encourage team members to internalize these changes more readily. Moreover, when managers exhibit genuine enthusiasm about new cultural elements, employees usually reciprocate with similar sentiments – thus accelerating the absorption process during a cultural shift.

The manager's engagement in open communication, prompt feedback, and recognition of efforts are practical strategies in enhancing their image. It can stimulate a sense of belonging among employees and encourage them to contribute constructively during a cultural shift. In the journey towards achieving cultural resonance, a manager's iconic image acts as a beacon guiding the way for the rest of the organization.

While it is common knowledge that an effective leader or manager is crucial to an organization's success - the underrated component is their iconic image. An iconic manager doesn't just manage cultural change—they inspire it. So, if your organization is looking to undertake a cultural shift, do not underestimate the implications of your manager's role and influence upon its successful implementation.

Factors impacting Cultural Shifts - Assessing & Influencing Organizational Culture

The cultural landscape of an organization is dynamic and ever-evolving. It continually undergoes minor and major shifts based on internal changes such as management style, team dynamics, vision alignment, and external influences like market trends or regulatory requirements. These shifts, although inevitable, need thorough planning and strategic execution to avoid any negative impact on the overall functioning of the organization.

Understanding this brings us to the critical aspects of assessing organizational culture and influencing organizational culture. Both these processes are essential in successfully managing changes in the cultural attitude within the establishment.

Assessing Organizational Culture:

To initiate a cultural shift in an organization, one must first understand its existing culture. The assessment involves studying observable features such as communication patterns, decision-making styles, work environment, leadership styles, employee motivation factors, and so on. Moreover, unobservable elements such as shared values, belief systems, assumptions also form an integral part of this assessment process. A thorough examination provides a clear understanding of what works well within the current culture and what requires change for better resonance.

A variety of approaches can be used to assess culture that includes surveys, interviews with staff members at different levels, observation of behavioral patterns etc. Also consider bringing in neutral third party experts who can provide a fresh perspective while assessing your organization's culture.

Influencing Organizational Culture:

Once you have assessed your current organizational culture comprehensively and identified areas that need improvement or change; the next step involves becoming an influencer for those changes. This means not only introducing potential changes but ensuring they are implemented successfully.

The mechanism through which cultural shifts can be influenced varies, largely depending on the nature and size of the organization. Smaller organizations might find it easier to implement changes due to fewer hierarchies and close-knit teams. On the other hand, larger corporations might need more time due to their complex structures.

Influencing a cultural shift requires transparent communication about why the change is necessary, what improvements it will bring, and how it aligns with the organization's overall objectives. Leaders should engage in an open dialogue, attending to questions or concerns raised by team members and ensuring them their opinions are valued during this transition phase.

Remember: cultural shifts aren't overnight initiatives but result from continuous effort and patience. So while influencing these shifts, leaders should also focus on building resilience among employees for change adaptations. Inclusion of training programs could help in this regard by preparing their team psychologically to accept new cultural norms.

Influencing culture also means that leaders are required to set examples through their behavior. They need to live out the changes they want to see within their organization because actions do speak louder than words. When employees see their leaders embracing change positively, they too find easier acceptance.

To summarize, assessing and influencing organizational culture are two critical aspects when it comes to managing cultural shifts within an establishment. They require strategic planning combined with empathetic leadership so as to successfully transit from one cultural paradigm to another without affecting employee morale or productivity adversely.

Strategies for Effective Cultural Resonance in Organizations

The journey towards achieving cultural resonance within an organization is indeed challenging. It requires meticulous planning, thoughtful execution and unyielding commitment from all members of the organization. However, through a well-crafted mix of strategies, you can capture and maintain cultural resonance effectively, no matter how daunting the task initially appears. The following are some tested and proven strategies that can guide your organization on the path to successful cultural shift.

Define Your Desired Culture:

The first step towards creating cultural resonance is defining the desired state of your organizational culture. This should ideally reflect your brand's vision, mission and values aligned with employee expectations and market realities. Articulating your ideal culture clearly will serve as a solid foundation upon which you can build resonance.

Communicate Openly and Frequently:

For cultural resonance to occur, open and frequent communication is vital. Communicating with clarity about why certain changes are needed, how they align with the company's vision, and what benefits they bring for both individuals and teams helps to foster understanding and gain buy-in from all members of the team.

Train & Develop Employees:

In implementing cultural shifts, investing in appropriate training and development programs for teams plays a key role in fostering cultural resonance. Such programs not only equip employees with new skills required but also assist them to understand their role in reinforcing new behaviors consistent with desired cultural attributes.

Showcase Success Stories:

Stories resonate deeply with people as they connect at an emotional level. Sharing stories or case studies highlighting employees who've successfully adapted to cultural changes can serve as inspiration for others. This way, you can leverage the power of storytelling to foster cultural resonance in your organization.

Lead by Example:

Leaders play a crucial role in bringing about cultural shifts. Leaders who lead by example and embody the desired culture are more likely to inspire others to follow suit. By walking their talk, leaders can cultivate a stronger sense of trust and commitment among their team members, leading to higher cultural resonance.

In conclusion, fostering cultural resonance within an organization is not a one-time activity but rather an ongoing process that requires consistent effort and reinforcement at all levels of the organization. By employing these strategies, you can ensure that your company's culture remains vibrant, relevant and resonates deeply with everyone involved thus guiding your organization towards greater success.

Fostering a Sense of Belonging & Pride Among Employees During Organizational Shifts

Any cultural shift within an organization implies change - and change can often be met with apprehension, resistance, or at the very least, uncertainty among employees. It's during this challenging phase of transition that fostering a sense of belonging and pride among employees becomes vitally important. Let's delve deeper into understanding how organizational leaders can create this sense of belonging and pride.

Cultivating a Sense of Belonging:

A sense of belonging within an organization refers to employees' perception of being part of the team. They feel valued for their unique contributions, respected for their ideas, and trusted as individuals. Cultivating this sense in the midst of cultural shifts starts with creating a culture that values diversity and inclusivity.

Giving every employee regardless of their role fair access to resources, opportunities and decision-making is critical. Encourage colleagues to support each other as they navigate through changes, promoting cohesion and mutual trust. Recognize individual efforts and achievements publicly – nothing fosters a stronger sense of belonging than feeling acknowledged.

Most importantly, maintain an open line of communication with all employees at every stage of implementing your cultural shift. Make sure they have an outlet to voice any concerns or queries regarding new procedures or standards established by the shift. When employees feel heard and supported in times of change, they're more likely to embrace new culture elements willingly.

Boosting Pride Among Employees:

Pride in the workplace is about instilling a collective sense of accomplishment among employees. Employees who take pride in their work are often happier, more engaged, and generally perform better.

You can foster pride among employees during a cultural shift by celebrating the successful implementation of new changes. Share key milestones achieved during the transition phase with all team members. Highlight how their collective efforts have contributed to realizing these milestones and let them know that their hard work is making a difference.

Another effective strategy is to integrate elements of the new culture into day-to-day operations. For example, if your cultural shift involves promoting sustainability, showcase how individual and collective actions are contributing towards this goal in tangible ways, like reduced resource wastage or increased energy efficiency. Highlighting such visible impacts can boost pride among employees as they witness the fruits of their commitment and diligence.

To sum up, fostering a sense of belonging and boosting pride among employees are two vital links in achieving cultural resonance. These factors contribute significantly towards building an engaged, motivated workforce that's not only accepting but deeply supportive of the organizational culture change.

Chapter **6**

Challenges on the Path
to Iconicity

Employee Empowerment through Iconic Leadership

The Psychology Behind Iconic Leadership

1. The Importance of Understanding Psychological Principles

In order to become an iconic leader, it is crucial to have a deep understanding of the psychological principles that drive employee motivation and inspire performance. By delving into these underlying principles, leaders can gain valuable insights into what truly motivates their team members and how to effectively tap into those motivations. This understanding allows leaders to tailor their leadership approach in a way that resonates with individuals on a deeper level, ultimately fostering a higher level of engagement and satisfaction within the team.

2. Tapping into Intrinsic Motivations

One of the key aspects of inspiring and motivating employees is tapping into their intrinsic motivations. Intrinsic motivation refers to the internal drives and desires that individuals have to engage in a particular activity for its own sake, rather than for external rewards or incentives. By understanding what truly motivates each team member at a personal level, leaders can create an environment that nurtures these intrinsic motivations.

To tap into intrinsic motivations, leaders should take the time to get to know their team members individually. By having open conversations and actively listening to their aspirations, passions, and values, leaders can gain valuable insights into what truly fuels each person's internal motivation. With this knowledge, leaders can then align individual goals and tasks with these intrinsic motivators, creating a sense of purpose and fulfillment within the team.

Additionally, recognizing and celebrating achievements that are personally meaningful to team members can also tap into intrinsic motivations. By acknowledging and appreciating their efforts, leaders can inspire a sense of pride and accomplishment, further fueling their intrinsic motivation.

3. The Role of Emotional Intelligence

Emotional intelligence plays a crucial role in iconic leadership as it enables leaders to effectively connect with and inspire their employees. Emotional intelligence refers to the ability to identify, understand, and manage one's own emotions, as well as recognize and empathize with the emotions of others.

By developing their emotional intelligence, leaders can foster stronger connections with their team members, creating a foundation of trust and respect. This emotional connection empowers leaders to better understand the needs, concerns, and aspirations of their employees, enabling them to tailor their leadership style accordingly.

To enhance emotional intelligence, leaders can focus on self-reflection and self-awareness. By understanding their own emotions and how they impact their interactions with others, leaders can better regulate their emotions in the workplace. Additionally, actively practicing empathy and active listening allows leaders to create an environment where team members feel valued and heard.

4. Creating a Positive Work Environment

A positive work environment is essential for inspiring and motivating employees. When individuals feel supported, valued, and encouraged, they are more likely to be engaged and motivated in their work. As an iconic leader, it is crucial to create such an environment within the team.

To foster a positive work environment, leaders should promote open communication and collaboration. Encouraging team members to express their ideas, opinions, and concerns freely creates a sense of psychological safety where individuals feel comfortable taking risks and sharing their thoughts. Recognizing and appreciating the contributions of each team member also plays a significant role in creating a positive atmosphere.

Moreover, setting clear expectations and providing feedback that focuses on growth and improvement rather than criticism helps foster a positive work culture. Leaders can also establish rituals or traditions that promote positivity, such as celebrating achievements or organizing team-building activities. By consistently prioritizing positivity, leaders can create an environment that inspires and motivates employees to perform at their best.

5. Overcoming Psychological Barriers

In the pursuit of inspiring and motivating employees, leaders may encounter various psychological barriers that hinder individual performance. These barriers can include fear of failure, lack of confidence, resistance to change, or feeling undervalued.

Leaders must address these barriers head-on by providing support and guidance to help team members overcome them. By fostering a culture of trust and psychological safety, leaders can create an environment where individuals feel comfortable seeking assistance and taking risks. Offering coaching and mentorship opportunities can provide additional support to those facing psychological barriers, helping them build confidence and develop new skills.

Leaders should also focus on cultivating a growth mindset within the team. Encouraging a belief in continuous learning and development can help individuals overcome self-doubt and embrace challenges. By fostering a supportive environment that prioritizes personal growth, leaders can empower their team members to push past psychological barriers and unlock their full potential.

By understanding the underlying psychological principles, tapping into intrinsic motivations, developing emotional intelligence, creating a positive work environment, and addressing psychological barriers, leaders can embrace their role as iconic figures who inspire and motivate their employees to reach new heights.

Unleashing Power: Iconic Leaders Sparking Employee Empowerment and Organizational Success

In the dynamic world of business, leadership is not a mere trait or title; it is an integral lifeline that can take an organization from average to exceptional. Among various leadership styles that exist, one stands out for its transformational potential - and that is Iconic Leadership.

Remember that iconic leaders are individuals who inspire, motivate, and command respect due to their unique capabilities, approach, vision, and charisma. They set themselves apart with their ability to convert vision into reality, motivate teams towards a common goal, and foster a culture of empowerment and inclusive growth within the organization. Such leaders leave an indelible impact on the people they lead, thereby shaping the overall destiny of the organization.

Yet what makes iconic leaders so critical for organizational success? Research and studies have pointed out some compelling reasons. According to a study by Gallup, businesses led by high-performing managers reported up to 48% higher profitability than those with average leaders. Another report by Deloitte emphasizes that leadership effectiveness contributes to 32% variance in employee engagement levels, directly affecting productivity and retention. Furthermore, a study by the Center for Creative Leadership discovered that organizations with superior leadership exhibited twice the revenue growth compared to those with weaker leadership.

Beyond these statistics, it's also essential to understand that iconic leaders aren't just born – they're cultivated. Businesses that prioritize building such leaders typically create a fertile environment conducive to growth, innovation, and resilience. Consider Apple's Steve Jobs or Microsoft's Bill Gates; these industry titans were acknowledged for their iconic leadership style. Their focus was not solely on driving profit but on fostering a culture of inspiration, creativity and empowerment among their workforce. This ultimately contributes immensely to organizational success.

To quote Peter Drucker, an iconic leader in the field of management, "Leadership is not about being in charge. It is about taking care of those in your charge." This underscores the profound impact an iconic leader can have on their organization and its people. They nurture an environment where employees feel valued and motivated to contribute their best towards the organization's goals.

Role of Iconic Leaders in Employee Empowerment & Motivation

Without doubt, iconic leaders have the potential to act as catalysts, driving employee motivation and empowerment. The question that arises is how do they achieve this potent influence? It boils down to a unique blend of behaviours and strategies that iconic leaders employ.

To begin with, such leaders inspire by setting a clear vision and sharing it passionately. They are not just 'doers', but also 'dreamers' who give their team something meaningful to aspire for. This vision acts as a motivational beacon, guiding employees through challenges they encounter in their path. Bridgette Hyacinth, an international keynote speaker on leadership and author of 'The Future of Leadership: Rise of Automation, Robotics and Artificial Intelligence' says "Leadership is about making others better as a result of your presence". Iconic leaders exemplify this sentiment by creating a positive ripple effect throughout their organizations.

In tandem with this inspirational component is the equally crucial aspect of empowerment. Iconic leaders empower their staff by entrusting them with responsibility and giving them autonomy over their tasks. They create a space where employees can make decisions, experiment and take calculated risks without fear of blame or punishment. Empowerment boosts not only employee's self-confidence but also fosters innovation and creativity within the workforce.

Case studies often bring these concepts to life more vividly than mere theory does. Take Richard Branson, the founder of Virgin Group, for instance. He has always endorsed an employee-centric approach to business - valuing his people above profit margins or growth metrics. His belief is that when an organization truly cares for its employees and motivates them towards fulfilling personal goals, they reciprocate with exemplary dedication towards the company's success.

A quote from Branson perfectly captures his philosophy: "Train people well enough so they can leave, treat them well enough so they don't want to." This outlook has fueled Virgin Group's phenomenal growth, from a small music store to a global conglomerate with over 400 companies. Even amidst this expansive diversification, the organization consistently maintains high employee satisfaction and engagement levels – a testament to the effectiveness of truly empowered leadership.

Another iconic leader who harnessed employee empowerment is Mary Barra, CEO of General Motors. Barra launched a company-wide initiative to simplify and streamline GM's 10-page dress code into two words: "Dress appropriately". This significant move demonstrated her trust in employees' judgment while empowering them with the responsibility of representing their brand professionally. Under her leadership, GM has witnessed increased employee morale, reduced bureaucracy and higher productivity.

Iconic leaders can substantially influence their organizations by strategically weaving motivation and empowerment into their leadership style. They masterfully balance between being visionary guides and enablers - inspiring their teams towards grand ambitions while simultaneously granting them the freedom to pursue these goals in their unique ways. The results are stronger alignment, increased initiative, enhanced innovation and better performance - all stepping stones towards greater organizational success.

Empowered Employees & Organizational Success – The Correlation

Having explored the defining characteristics of iconic leaders and their transformational influence on employee empowerment and motivation, it is equally important to understand how these factors contribute directly to organizational success. The correlation between employee empowerment and organizational success has been researched extensively, with results demonstrating a positive, symbiotic relationship.

In simple terms, empowered employees are given the freedom and capacity to make decisions related to their work without needing explicit approval from their superiors. They have a sense of autonomy which leads them to feel more invested in and accountable for their work outcomes. This sense of ownership often translates into increased dedication, initiative, creativity, and productivity - all crucial elements driving organizational success.

A study conducted by Harvard Business Review discovered that companies that excelled at customer experience had 1.5 times more engaged employees than those with less satisfactory customer experience. This indicates that there is an inherent link between engaged (and in turn empowered) employees and satisfied customers. Satisfaction amongst customers can lead to repeat business and positive word-of-mouth marketing, both of which contribute significantly towards increased profitability for organizations.

Beyond these tangible benefits, empowered employees also contribute positively towards creating a culture that fosters continuous improvement. As they are encouraged to experiment and take calculated risks, they become natural innovators who constantly seek new ways to enhance efficiency or quality of the organization's products or services.

To put things into perspective, consider the example of Google, a company widely known for its unique work environment and high levels of employee engagement. One key policy that Google implemented was the '20% time' rule which allowed employees to spend 20% of their time working on personal projects that they believe could have value for the company. This policy led to the creation of some of Google's most successful products like Gmail and Google News. The policy demonstrated the company's trust in their employees' creative capabilities, thereby empowering them to innovate.

Furthermore, Southwest Airlines, a trailblazer in employee empowerment, attributes its sustained profitability to its robust culture of employee engagement. Their philosophy is simple: "Happy Employees = Happy Customers". They have established a name for going the extra mile in recognizing and rewarding employee efforts - leading to high morale, outstanding customer service and by extension, increased customer loyalty.

Organizations that prioritize and foster employee empowerment create a positive ripple effect which fuels higher productivity levels, enhanced innovation, superior customer satisfaction and ultimately leads to sustainable organizational success. Iconic leaders play an indispensable role in this equation as they are the ones who inspire, enable and nurture such an environment of autonomy and growth.

Creating a Cycle of Continuous Improvement and Development

The commitment to continuous improvement and employee development is a hallmark of iconic leaders. It creates a culture that encourages constant learning, innovation, and performance enhancement, resulting in overall organizational success. An effective tool in fostering such an environment is the implementation of a productive feedback loop.

An efficient feedback loop involves setting clear expectations, observing performance, providing constructive feedback to employees, and then refining the strategies based on the results. This system motivates employees to strive for better performance while at the same time provides a mechanism to implement necessary improvements.

Mary Kay Ash, founder of Mary Kay Cosmetics, known for her empowering leadership style once said, "Pretend that every single person you meet has a sign around his or her neck that says, 'Make me feel important.' Not only will you succeed in sales, you will succeed in life." A positive feedback loop is one way to make employees feel valued as it shows that their efforts are recognized and appreciated.

Incorporating regular feedback sessions helps iconic leaders identify any gaps in performance and address them promptly. These leaders understand the importance of open communication channels within their organization. They encourage their team members to express their views freely and give their input on decision-making processes. This contributes towards creating an empowered work environment wherein employees are not passive receivers but active participants in shaping organizational strategy.

A great example of the power of continuous improvement comes from Toyota's famed production system which includes the principle of 'Kaizen' or continuous improvement. The philosophy suggests that everyone from top management to assembly line workers should come up with small suggestions on a regular basis to improve productivity, quality and reduce waste. This idea defines some of the world's most successful businesses today!

The concept of Kaizen and lean manufacturing was subsequently adopted by other companies such as Ford and General Motors, leading to significant improvements in their operations. The constant feedback loop established between supervisors and workers in these companies has played a vital role in keeping them at the forefront of innovation.

Furthermore, continuous improvement practices underpin Google's work culture where employees are encouraged to dedicate 20% of their time on projects that they believe might benefit Google. This not only leads to exciting new ideas but also promotes a culture of empowerment and growth.

In conclusion, iconic leaders view continuous improvement not as an option, but as a strategic necessity. By adopting effective feedback mechanisms and investing in the development of employees, they empower their workforce to reach its full potential. Through this approach, iconic leaders create an agile organization that is ever-evolving, constantly improving, and consistently outperforming competition. With each enhancement made, there is a positive impact on efficiency, customer satisfaction, staff retention and ultimately organizational success.

Impactful Strategies & Techniques of Iconic Leaders

Iconic leaders stand apart from the crowd due to their distinctive strategies and techniques. These leaders go beyond the conventional norms and manifest a unique blend of transformative actions that foster employee empowerment, instill motivation, and drive organizational success.

A crucial aspect of iconic leadership is promoting transparency within the organization. Iconic leaders ensure that all employees understand the company's objectives, plans and expectations clearly. By fostering open communication channels, these leaders make sure that every team member feels included in the big picture. This sense of inclusivity leads to higher levels of engagement, trust and motivation among the workforce.

Another impactful technique used by iconic leaders is coaching. Unlike traditional leadership where orders are typically given top-down, iconic leaders take an active interest in developing their team members' skills and capacities. They coach their teams towards achieving excellence, offering constructive criticism along with encouragement and support. Additionally, they create opportunities for continual learning through programs, workshops or seminars in order to further enhance their teams' potential.

Take Microsoft's CEO Satya Nadella as an example of iconic leadership. When Nadella took over Microsoft's reins in 2014, he not only changed the company's strategic direction but also its culture. Nadella implemented a "growth mindset" approach encouraging employees to learn from mistakes instead of fearing them. This shift from a "know-it-all" culture to a "learn-it-all" culture rejuvenated Microsoft's innovative spirit thus driving strong business results.

Besides transparency and coaching, iconic leaders also show empathy – caring about their employees as individuals beyond just work resources. By acknowledging their personal interests, concerns or challenges, these leaders cultivate a supportive work environment where individuals feel valued and recognized as human beings rather than merely cogs in a machine.

An exceptional example of such empathetic leadership is Indra Nooyi, the former CEO of PepsiCo. Known for her humane leadership style, Nooyi ensured she wrote over 400 letters annually to the parents of her top senior executives expressing gratitude for their integral role in her team's success. This unique initiative did wonders for employee morale and pride.

Furthermore, iconic leaders keep their teams inspired and engaged through their undeterred resilience in adversity. They set an example by showing courage in the face of setbacks thereby encouraging their teams to persevere despite challenges.

A case study worth mentioning here is of Steve Jobs, co-founder of Apple. Despite being ousted from his own company, Jobs never lost sight of his vision or purpose. His resilience led him back to Apple where he ushered in a new era of innovation with products like iPods, iPhones and iPads which revolutionized the tech industry. Jobs' comeback story has since inspired many business leaders around the world.

The bottom line is that every iconic leader may have a unique way of steering their organization but all possess a common trait - they value and empower their employees. By fostering communicative transparency, providing continual coaching, exhibiting empathy and demonstrating resilience in adversity; these leaders not only motivate but also inspire employees to contribute to broader organizational success.

Chapter 7

Sustaining Iconicity

Establishing a lasting and impactful leadership image is paramount in today's corporate landscape. It carries the power to inspire teams, drive transformational changes, and scale professional heights. However, this journey is far from straightforward. As one embarks on this path, they encounter unique challenges, including resistance and skepticism among peers and subordinates, handling setbacks, and adapting one's leadership approach for improved resilience.

"Realistic exploration of challenges faced in establishing an iconic leadership image" might seem like a mouthful, but it essentially boils down to understanding what separates leaders that are simply remembered from those that become iconic. What makes their leadership style unique? What hurdles do they face, and how do they rise above them? This section aims to answer these questions and more, providing readers with strategies and insights into crafting their leadership narrative.

The corporate world is brimming with stories of great leaders who have navigated through challenging circumstances to leave an indelible imprint on their organizations. Steve Jobs encouraged 'thinking differently,' Angela Merkel embodies resilience under pressure, while Indra Nooyi is known for her advocacy for work-life balance. Despite their different sectors and styles, they all share one commonality – an iconic leadership image that is respected and admired. Through this section, we will deconstruct the key components of such esteemed leadership images and offer practical advice for aspiring leaders.

Our discussion focuses on three main pillars - first, establishing a strong leadership image; second, dealing with skepticism and resistance within the team; third, using setbacks as stepping stones to success rather than deterrents. These subjects aren't just talking points; instead, they serve as guiding themes that provide structure to our conversation about realistic leadership development.

To give you a sense of what's ahead, we'll delve into each of these themes in detail. We'll talk about the crucial elements for cultivating a leadership image that resonates with both your team and the external world. We'll explore proven strategies for overcoming resistance and skepticism within your team, fostering an atmosphere of mutual respect and cooperation. And lastly, we'll discuss how to learn from setbacks and adapt your leadership style for resilience, ensuring you not only bounce back from challenges but also emerge stronger.

To conclude this introduction, here's your hook: Becoming an iconic leader is not about being infallible or getting it right every time. It's about embracing imperfections, taking calculated risks, and continually learning and growing. So, if you're ready to evolve your leadership approach and make a remarkable difference in the lives of those led by you, keep reading. This may just be the section that catalyzes your journey from being a good leader to becoming an iconic one.

Establishing Leadership Image

In leading towards triumph, the first major step is establishing a captivating leadership image. This may seem like an elusive goal, but it's essentially about creating a consistent identity that people trust and respect. Your leadership image is the perception you generate in others' minds—your peers, subordinates, or even competitors. Let's look at some elements that can help you create this image.

Communication Style: Effective communication forms the axis on which the wheel of leadership spins. As they say, it's not just about what you communicate but also how you do it. A reliable leader communicates with clarity and decisiveness, facilitating understanding and instigating necessary actions.

"Leadership challenges faced in establishing an iconic image" often revolve around mastering this art of communication. It requires balancing directness with empathy and authoritative speeches with active listening. For example, Satya Nadella, Microsoft CEO, is known for his empathetic communication style that has shaped the company's culture of inclusivity.

Empathy: Empathetic leaders resonate well within teams because they understand their members' perspectives and feelings. They foster a sense of belonging and motivate team members to perform better. When leaders reflect empathy in their behavior, they establish an image of being accessible and approachable.

Leaders who display genuine empathy tend to build more robust and meaningful connections within their team. Their empathetic demeanour also aids in "overcoming resistance and skepticism" within the team by making subordinates feel valued and understood.

Problem-solving Approach: The manner in which a leader approaches problem-solving situations plays a significant role in shaping their leadership image. Leaders should possess analytical acumen to assess problems accurately and encourage innovative solutions, thereby fostering a culture of creativity and flexibility. Let's take Elon Musk, for example. He is applauded for his innovative problem-solving approach that has revolutionized space exploration and electric cars.

Adopting a Resilient Attitude: A leader's response to adversity is another crucial element in establishing an iconic leadership image. As John C. Maxwell once said, "The pessimist complains about the wind. The optimist expects it to change. The leader adjusts the sails." Resilient leaders adapt quickly, remain optimistic amid setbacks, and exhibit unwavering determination to achieve their objectives. Such leaders inspire their teams to face challenges head-on and bounce back from failures.

In conclusion, establishing an iconic leadership image demands a blend of effective communication, empathy towards team members, a creative problem-solving mindset, and resilience in the face of adversity—a hefty toolbox indeed! However, remember that becoming an iconic leader is not about perfectionism but progressivism. Approach each day as a chance for growth and learning, and soon enough, you will see your leadership image evolve into one that commands respect and inspires others.

Overcoming Resistance and Skepticism

Navigating the labyrinth of leadership isn't solely about personal growth; it also involves fostering a culture of trust and acceptance within your team. It's no secret that change, even when positive, can birth resistance and skepticism among team members. Being able to address these feelings effectively is an integral aspect of being an effective leader.

A closer look at "*Realistic exploration of challenges faced in establishing an iconic leadership image*" reveals that one major impediment leaders confront is resistance from their own team. Resistance can stem from numerous factors – fear of change, lack of understanding about why changes are necessary or simple inertia. Regardless of the source, it's pivotal for a leader to address and overcome this resistance proactively.

Leading with empathy plays a crucial role here. Empathetic leaders, who make an effort to understand their team's concerns and fears, are more likely to alleviate resistance and build support. Inclusion is key – when people feel that their opinions matter, they're less likely to resist decisions. Encourage open dialogue within your team and focus on creating an environment where every voice counts.

In addition to empathy, clear and transparent communication is another powerful tool for overcoming resistance. Leaders should take pains to explain not just what changes are being implemented but also why those changes are necessary and how they would benefit the team in the long run. Providing this context helps demystify changes and quell unfounded worries or fears.

Now let us shift our gaze towards another challenge – skepticism. Skepticism within a team, while healthy in moderate amounts as it encourages critical thinking, can become problematic if left unchecked. When skepticism starts breeding negativity or hindering progress, leaders need to step in decisively.

Conquering skepticism begins with establishing credibility, which is often a byproduct of consistency in action and behavior. As the saying goes, "actions speak louder than words." Leaders who consistently walk their talk demonstrate reliability and authenticity, which are key to combating skepticism. Actively seek feedback and be open to criticism. Showing that you value different opinions creates an atmosphere of mutual respect and builds credibility.

"*Overcoming resistance and skepticism within the team*" may seem like a daunting task, but with persistence, empathy, clear communication, and credible actions, leaders can turn these challenges into opportunities for growth and cohesion within the team.

In conclusion, building an iconic leadership image isn't just about sculpting your own persona. It's also about how you transform adversity into opportunity, address resistance and skepticism within your team constructively, and nurture a culture of trust. Remember that the journey to becoming an iconic leader is as much about paving the path for others as it is about self-improvement.

Embracing and Learning from Setbacks

The journey to becoming an iconic leader is steeped in challenges, with the most formidable of them being setbacks. A setback can be viewed as a failure or a situation where desired results aren't realized despite one's best efforts. "*Learning from setbacks*" is not just about resilience; it is also about pinpointing what went wrong and using that knowledge to avoid similar pitfalls in the future.

Framing Setbacks Positively: The first step towards learning from a setback is framing it positively. A negative view can cloud judgment and hinder growth, while a positive perspective fosters learning. As Winston Churchill once said, "Success is not final, failure is not fatal: It is the courage to continue that counts." Viewing setbacks as stepping stones rather than stumbling blocks paves the way for continuous learning and improvement.

Root Cause Analysis: In order to understand what led to the setback, conducting root cause analysis is essential. This involves identifying contributing factors and analyzing them critically. Honest introspection often yields valuable insights that can guide corrective actions and future decisions.

Adapting Leadership Approach: Another crucial part of *"learning from setbacks"* involves adapting your leadership style based on the lessons learned. For instance, if a strategy fails due to lack of team involvement or resistance from members, it may signal that incorporating more inclusivity or addressing fears more effectively could be beneficial.

One must remember though, adapting does not mean compromising on core values or leadership vision. Instead, it demands flexibility in approach without losing sight of one's goals.

Leveraging Support Systems: Embracing setbacks also means leveraging support systems effectively during tough times - whether it be mentors, peers or even team members. They can offer fresh perspectives, help navigate challenging situations and provide necessary encouragement.

Consider the journey of Steve Jobs, a paragon of leadership triumphing over adversity. When he was forced to leave Apple, instead of viewing it as a failure, he framed it as an opportunity for personal growth. He later founded NeXT computers and Pixar Animation Studios which were massively successful ventures. His setback at Apple was instrumental in crafting these successes.

Instilling Resilience in the Team: Lastly, your reaction to setbacks as a leader plays a significant role in shaping your team's attitude towards failures. Leaders who handle setbacks with grace and resilience set an example for their teams to do the same. Constructive approach towards failures and determination to learn from them fosters a culture where mistakes are viewed not as obstacles but opportunities for growth.

In conclusion, setbacks are inevitable in any leadership journey. What sets iconic leaders apart is how they view these setbacks and what they learn from them. Always remember that in every setback lies a setup for an incredible comeback!

Building Resilience and Adaptation in Leadership

The path towards iconic leadership isn't paved with just success stories, it is also marked by the ability to bounce back from adversities, adapt to changing situations, and instill resilience within the team. How a leader responds to challenges often shapes their legacy far more than their victories. In the words of American author and motivational speaker Zig Ziglar,"Difficult roads often lead to beautiful destinations."

Leading with Resilience: One of the first steps in *"adapting leadership approach"* centers on building resilience. A resilient leader does not merely survive hardships but thrives amidst them. They display courage in adverse situations, maintain equilibrium during periods of uncertainty, and inspire optimism across the team.

The story of Angela Merkel, the German Chancellor, is an inspiring example of such resilience. Despite various political upheavals and crises during her tenure, she stood firm, leading

Germany through some extraordinarily challenging times. It's her resilience that has made her one of the world's most powerful leaders.

Cultivating Adaptability: Alongside resilience, adaptability is equally crucial for successful leadership. Times change and so do circumstances; static leadership styles can often become obsolete or ineffective under these changing conditions. Therefore, it's essential for a leader to remain receptive to new ideas, open to experimentation and unafraid of altering course when necessary.

Jeff Bezos aptly illustrates this notion of adaptation and flexibility. Recognizing early-on the potential of the internet led him to launch Amazon initially as an online bookstore, which eventually evolved into the world's largest online marketplace under his adaptable leadership.

Weathering Storms: Another important aspect of adapting your leadership approach revolves around managing crisis situations or significant changes. These are times when a leader's mettle is seriously tested. Crisis demands swift and effective decisions that can determine the future course of the organization.

Leadership resilience is vital here, not just to stay afloat during turbulent times but also to navigate through them successfully, learning valuable lessons along the way. "*Leadership setbacks*", "*team resistance*", "*team skepticism*" - all these challenges can be better managed when viewed from a lens of resilience and adaptability.

Inspiring Resilience in Teams: Being resilient yourself is important, but instilling the same characteristic within your team is equally crucial. Iconic leaders create an environment that promotes learning from failures rather than fearing them. Encouraging team members to push their boundaries, take calculated risks and bounce back from setbacks fosters a collective sense of resilience.

In conclusion, building resilience and adaptation into your leadership approach doesn't mean avoiding difficulties or seeking an easy path. It embodies learning from adversities, adapting one's strategies in alignment with changing scenarios, and inspiring teams to do the same. This approach not only makes you more resilient as a leader but also cultivates resilience within your team, paving way for long-term growth and success.

Chapter 8

Mastering the Art of Inclusive Iconicity: Build a Diverse, Iconic Leadership That Resonates

One of the hottest topics in management circles today is The Art of Inclusive Iconicity, an approach that emphasizes iconic leadership built on diversity and inclusion. This concept is not just an abstract, fancy term; it is fast becoming a necessary part of how organizations thrive in a progressively global and diverse society. So, what exactly does *Inclusive Iconicity* entail? And why is it increasingly crucial for business leaders?

Inclusive Iconicity blends two essential components: iconic leadership and diversity inclusion. *Iconic leadership* refers to a leadership style that carries symbolic power, inspires admiration and respect, and significantly influences its environment. It's about leaders carving out distinctively memorable images through their actions and characteristics. What makes this iconic status especially noteworthy today, is when it encompasses diversity and inclusion.

Now, let's talk about *diversity and inclusion*. Diversity in the workplace no longer merely represents a mix of gender, race, or nationality. It now extends to a wide range of factors such as age, social background, experiences, skills, perspectives, and other human facets. Inclusion, on the other hand, means that these differences are genuinely acknowledged and celebrated within the organization. An inclusive workplace enables every individual to feel valued, heard, respected, and empowered.

When combined effectively — iconic leadership with diversity and inclusion results in *The Art of Inclusive Iconicity*. Every member of the workforce sees a part of themselves mirrored in their leaders. As such, they feel more connected to those at the helm— boosting motivation, engagement, collaboration, and ultimately productivity.

The advantages of mastering this art extend beyond mere optics or checking the proverbial 'diversity' box. A diverse team brings a plethora of ideas, experiences, and perspectives that can spur innovation and problem-solving. On the other hand, leaders who embody iconic status combined with inclusive values can resonate more profoundly with their diverse team members. This harmony cultivates a sense of belonging, cohesiveness, and mutual respect — driving both employee satisfaction and business success.

But achieving Inclusive Iconicity isn't as simple as adopting a new policy or hosting diversity training sessions. It requires a deep-seated commitment from leadership, a strategic approach to nurturing diversity, and active engagement in fostering inclusion at all levels. And even then, it's not a destination but a continuous journey marked by learning, growth, and refinement.

As we delve deeper into this discussion, you'll gain insights into how to fully embrace diversity and inclusion, practical strategies for expressing inclusive iconicity, resonating with all team members, navigating potential challenges associated with fostering diversity and inclusivity, and cultivating an environment where everyone truly feels they belong.

The Imperative of Embracing Diversity and Inclusion

In the constantly evolving global business landscape, embracing diversity and inclusion isn't just a nice-to-have guiding principle—it's an absolute necessity. Any leadership aspiring to be iconic must recognize this imperative and weave it into the very fabric of their organizational culture.

Diverse teams breathe creativity and innovation—they function as melting pots of varied experiences, unique perspectives, rich knowledge, and distinct skillsets. By tapping into this wealth of resources, businesses can unlock innovative solutions to complex problems that a homogeneous group might miss. The Harvard Business Review points out in one study that diverse teams out-innovate and out-perform others. As such, diversity in the workplace ceases to be a mere buzzword; instead, it becomes a powerful driver of competitiveness and success.

However, having a diverse workforce is only beneficial if there is inclusion. Without genuine inclusivity, diversity runs the risk of being superficial—appearing progressive on paper while being stagnant in practice. A truly inclusive work environment ensures all individuals feel valued for their unique attributes without fear of alienation or marginalization. It fosters a sense of belonging among employees enabling them to contribute their best selves freely and safely.

Inclusive leadership, therefore, calls for managers who not only accommodate differences but also leverage these variations as strengths. These leaders engage with team members on an individual level, appreciate varied perspectives, promote equitable opportunities for growth, and cultivate an empathetic understanding of individual needs. They play an essential role in creating an atmosphere where everyone feels respected, heard, and empowered—breeding job satisfaction, loyalty, greater productivity, and ultimately positive bottom-line impacts.

Moreover, embracing diversity has compelling moral implications too. It's about fairness and equity, ensuring that all individuals, irrespective of their backgrounds, have the chance to thrive. More than just a matter of social justice, it's about respecting and valifying differences—encouraging pluralism and combating discrimination.

Finally, there's an irrefutable business case for embracing diversity. Companies with strong diversity metrics are shown to be more likely to capture new markets and improve customer orientation. They enjoy higher revenues, market shares, and profit margins as per a McKinsey study. Another comprehensive review by Boston Consulting Group found that companies with more diverse management teams generate nearly 20% higher revenue due to innovation. In today's interconnected global economy, businesses cannot afford to alienate potential customers based on nationality, ethnicity, gender, age, or any other parameter.

In conclusion, embracing diversity in every aspect—from hiring policies and training programs to corporate values and top leadership—isn't just the right thing to do; it makes sound business sense too. Combined with an inclusive leadership style that truly resonates at every level of the organization—it paves the way for thriving in the ever-challenging world of business.

Strategies for Expressing Inclusive Iconicity

Having grasped the importance of embracing diversity and inclusion, our next logical step is to understand practical strategies for expressing inclusive iconicity. An iconic status that pairs a manager's leadership prowess with their commitment to inclusivity can yield extraordinary results within an organization. Here are several strategies to enable leaders in becoming models of inclusive iconicity.

1. Creating an Inclusive Culture: For any organization, culture is everything. It drives conduct, shapes decision-making processes, and impacts how employees engage with their work and each other. Leaders play a crucial role in shaping this culture by integrating inclusive values into nearly every aspect of their organization's operations. This includes setting expectations about respectful communication, acceptance of diverse ideas, and promoting a collaborative environment where different perspectives can coalesce into innovative solutions.

2. Building an Inclusive Team: The success of any team often lies in its composition - combining individuals with varied skill-sets, experiences, backgrounds, and perspectives. As a leader seeking to build an inclusive team, mindfully selecting diverse individuals should be one priority. Then comes creating engagement platforms where everyone has equal opportunities to contribute their insights and learn from each other's experiences. Consequently, fostering an atmosphere of shared understanding and respect borne out of these interactions.

3. Emphasizing Personal Values: An iconic leader is not just about outward appearances or actions; it also entails personal attitudes towards diversity and inclusivity. Such leaders need to demonstrate through their words and actions that they appreciate diversity and genuinely believe in the power of inclusion. This encourages others to follow suit, thereby creating a ripple effect that permeates the entire organization.

4. Offering Equal Opportunities: In an inclusive leadership ecosystem, opportunities for growth are accessible to all, regardless of their diverse backgrounds. Leaders can ensure this by setting up fair and transparent processes for promotions, recognitions, and professional development. They need to actively work towards eliminating any systemic biases or barriers that might prevent certain groups from accessing these opportunities.

5. Open Communication: Establishing an open-door policy where team members feel free to share their thoughts, ideas, concerns and even perceived challenges will foster trust within the team. Leaders should also be intentional about understanding and acknowledging their own unconscious biases that could inadvertently affect how they communicate with or perceive others.

6. Providing Feedback and Encouragement: Feedback is a powerful tool in shaping behavior and encouraging growth. Giving each team member individual attention—highlighting strengths, discussing areas for improvements, offering guidance, and appreciating contributions—creates a supportive environment that motivates individuals, irrespective of who they are.

Effective application of these strategies can significantly enhance a leader's iconic status. However, it is important to remember that expressing inclusive iconicity isn't about one-time actions or grand gestures; it's about consistently demonstrating commitment towards diversity inclusion in every interaction with your team members.

Resonating with All Team Members

A core dimension of Inclusive Iconicity is the ability to resonate with all team members. This means transcending surface differences to connect with every individual on a humanistic level, honoring their unique experiences and perspectives. When leaders can accomplish this resonance, it fosters strong relationships across the team, cultivates a high-trust environment, boosts engagement, and enhances overall productivity.

The process of resonating with all team members begins by understanding that people are not one-dimensional. Each person brings diverse attributes and experiences to the table— from different cultural backgrounds, lifestyles, skills, and perspectives which are integral assets for innovation and decision-making in a diverse work environment.

Crucial to resonating with your diverse team is effective communication. Leaders need to master the art of communicating in ways that resonate with everyone on the team. The words you choose matter; so too does your tone of voice and body language. Effective communication involves active listening, expressing empathy, encouraging feedback, and staying open-minded.

Inclusive leadership, by its very nature demands that leaders strive to create a judgement-free zone within their teams where everyone feels secure to share ideas or concerns openly without fear of ridicule or reprisal. A leader who can make individuals feel heard will see an increase in trustworthiness among their team members, thus fostering stronger relationships.

A crucial strategy here is regular one-on-one interactions — yes it may be time-consuming but it allows for addressing specific needs and concerns. It also gives a clear impression that you consider each employee's contribution valuable irrespective of background or business rank. This cannot be overstated enough as employees are known to perform better when they know their leaders value them individually.

To truly resonate with every member of the team, leaders also need to demonstrate an understanding and respect for cultural differences. This may mean taking the time to learn more about various cultures represented within your team or making reasonable accommodations to account for different customs and traditions. Demonstrating this understanding helps build a greater sense of respect among diverse team members, leading to better teamwork and lesser misunderstandings.

Lastly, inclusive iconicity comes with recognizing and affirmatively acting upon biases—be they conscious or unconscious. Leaders must self-assess regularly; seeking feedback from diverse voices in their teams can be extremely beneficial since it's difficult to identify unwarranted biases by oneself. Once identified, immediate steps should be taken to challenge and overcome these prejudices.

In conclusion, being able to resonate with all team members is more than just being well-liked or popular. It's about forging deep connections based on mutual respect and understanding with your team members. It's about creating an environment where people feel valued, understood, and integrated into the organizational tapestry despite their varied backgrounds.

Navigating Challenges of Inclusive Iconicity

In the journey towards cultivating **Inclusive Iconicity**, it is undeniable that managers may encounter various challenges. Despite its many benefits, fostering a diverse and inclusive atmosphere is not without complexities. Successfully navigating these hurdles is integral to building an iconic status that truly resonates with a diverse team.

One significant challenge is dealing with inherent biases—both at the individual and organizational level. Bias often operates subtly and can be deeply ingrained. Unconscious biases may hinder fair decision-making processes and create unseen barriers for certain groups of employees. A leader aspiring for iconic status must identify these biases, counteract their impact, and work tirelessly to ensure all individuals are treated equitably.

<blockquote>Overcoming diversity challenges</blockquote> requires deliberate action, like facilitating bias awareness training or conducting regular audits of your practices to root out potential systemic bias.

Another common challenge in embracing diversity and inclusion is addressing the fear of conflict which can arise from differences. Diverse teams naturally have varied experiences, viewpoints, and communication styles. While this heterogeneity can drive innovation and creativity, it also has the potential to lead to misunderstandings or conflicts if not handled properly. The key here lies in promoting open dialogue, encouraging constructive disagreement, and modeling respectful conflict-resolution strategies.

Moreover, implementing inclusive practices and transforming organizational culture takes time; it doesn't happen overnight. Leaders may face resistance during this transformation process—be it from people accustomed to traditional ways of operation or those who view changes as threats rather than opportunities.

To navigate such resistance, patience paired with consistent effort will play big roles; explaining the benefits of diversity and inclusion frequently, providing reassurance regarding valid apprehensions about change, involving everyone in the transformation journey, or celebrating small wins can be effective strategies. It's important to constantly reiterate that practicing Inclusive Iconicity is not just a passing trend but an ongoing commitment towards better leadership and organizational success.

Inclusivity may also challenge conventional norms of leadership. Some leaders might fear they might lose their authority or respect by creating space for diverse voices, allowing dissent, or engaging in shared decision-making. However, inclusive leadership enhances rather than diminishes a leader's iconic status. Leaders who can draw on diverse talents, inspire inclusive innovation, and foster a sense of belonging among employees tend to be more highly respected and influential.

Navigating these challenges requires courage, perseverance, and a genuine commitment to diversity and inclusion. While it does present unique obstacles, the resulting outcomes—enhanced creativity, improved performance, higher employee satisfaction— are undeniably worth the effort.

Chapter 9

Iconic Listening: Transforming Leadership by Amplifying Employee Voices

In recent years, a new concept is taking center stage in leadership discussions: *Iconic Listening*. This practice goes beyond merely hearing employees to genuinely pursuing an understanding of their perspectives and experiences. It's not just about noting nod-and-smile narratives, but also decoding the unsaid and acknowledging diverse viewpoints. These are integral aspects of iconic leadership that underscore the importance of listening.

Iconic listening is one of the key elements that distinguishes successful leaders from others. With growing recognition of its impact on organizations, it isn't surprising that more emphasis is being placed on its significance in fostering an inclusive, respectful, and productive work environment. The right practices can empower individuals and teams, instigate creativity, and foster innovative thought ideas.

Active listening in leadership is at the heart of iconic listening. It's about engaging with employees in a way that assures them their voices are not merely heard but truly valued. Active listeners acknowledge feedback with empathy, allowing for open communication and dialogue. It's this kind of communication that builds trust within teams and leads to exceptional results.

The importance of listening in iconic leadership cannot be overstated. It bridges gaps between hierarchies, promotes inclusivity, enhances employee motivation, and contributes to creating workplaces where every voice matters. By inviting diverse voices into decision-making processes, leaders are able to drive innovation and ensure their strategies align with the needs and aspirations of their employees. This approach often leads to improved performance, increased engagement, and strong team dynamics.

Leaders practicing iconic leadership through active listening understand that every discussion is an opportunity for growth and learning - for themselves and their organization. By actively inviting, acknowledging, and acting on feedback, these leaders build an environment that promotes learning and growth.

Simply put, iconic listening is about valuing employee voices in every decision and action. It's this ethos that forms the foundation of an inclusive, productive, and creative workplace where employees feel valued and leaders are highly effective.

Describe How Feedback Mechanisms Enhance Understanding of Employee Needs

Recognizing and acknowledging employee voices is a cornerstone of iconic listening, yet the essential question remains: How can leaders truly understand the needs and aspirations of their employees? The answer lies in developing robust feedback mechanisms.

Feedback mechanisms are systems put in place by organizations to gather insights from their employees. They include regular surveys, town hall meetings, one-on-one discussions, suggestion boxes, or virtual feedback platforms. These avenues allow leaders to tap into the diverse perspectives within their organization and gain an accurate understanding of their employees' experiences.

Feedback mechanisms for employee needs serve a dual purpose. On one hand, they allow employees to express their views, opinions, ideas, and concerns openly. On the other hand, they provide invaluable data for management that guides decision-making processes.

The key here is ensuring these feedback channels are easily accessible and genuinely encourage participation. It's also crucial that employees feel safe expressing their thoughts without fear of backlash or judgment. When implemented correctly, these mechanisms foster a culture of open dialogue and enhance overall organizational transparency.

However, gathering feedback represents only half the equation. What sets iconic leaders apart is how they act on this information. Truly understanding and addressing employee needs through listening requires both empathy and action.

A forward-thinking leader doesn't just listen - they seek to understand the implications behind each piece of feedback received. By doing so, they can make informed decisions designed to meet those needs head-on or address concerns promptly.

An example might be an issue concerning workload balance brought up during a feedback session. While it may initially seem like a minor complaint about time allocation, further probing might reveal underlying issues related to resource allocation or process inefficiency. An iconic leader would acknowledge this, dig deeper, and implement changes that address the root cause.

Furthermore, actively communicating feedback outcomes back to employees is a critical step in the feedback loop. This action reinforces the notion that their voices are not only heard but are an instrumental part of organizational change. It's a primary way feedback mechanism amplify employee voices, driving meaningful business transformation while fostering a sense of ownership among staff.

In conclusion, effective feedback mechanisms play an important role in understanding and addressing employee needs through listening. They provide an essential touchpoint for employees to share their perspectives, experiences, and ideas directly with leadership. More importantly, by valuing these voices and acting upon their feedback, leaders can create workplaces where inclusivity isn't just a goal - it's a reality.

Elevating Employee Voices through Active Listening

The proverbial seat at the table is something that employees across organizations yearn for - to feel heard, to be noticed, and to know that their opinions matter. As leaders, how do we make this possible? The answer lies in elevating employee voices through the power of active listening.

Active listening in leadership is not merely about acknowledging a message; it's about comprehending its essence and seeing things from another person's perspective. It involves communicating understanding back to the speaker, ensuring they feel genuinely heard and valued. This invariably raises their voice in the organization.

Leaders who master elevating employee voices in leadership see a profound ripple effect across their organization—increased job satisfaction, enhanced trust between employees and management, improved team cohesiveness, higher innovation levels, and much more.

In practice, actively elevating employee voices can include practices like inviting contributions from all team members during meetings. This way, even employees who might otherwise remain quiet are encouraged to share their ideas. Emphasizing open-door policy for feedback or concerns can also play a key role.

The impact of amplifying employee voices through listening also extends beyond internal dynamics. By leading with empathy and understanding, companies can foster greater loyalty among their staff – an invaluable asset in today's competitive job market.

A common question may arise here: Does this approach risk consensus paralysis? Will decision-making become inefficient with too many voices included? Not necessarily. Paralysis typically results from a lack of decision-making authority or unclear roles and responsibilities - not open communication. As long as expectations are established upfront concerning input solicitation versus decision-making authority, companies can avoid such pitfalls.

Taking cues from iconic leaders around the world, honing your active listening abilities further could involve participatively designing solutions with those affected. Essentially, instead of dictating changes, leaders co-create them with their team - a testament to both democratic leadership and the power of collective creativity.

Leaders need to be ready for constructive criticism too. The point of elevating employee voices in leadership is not just to hear praise or ideas that align with your existing thought processes. Actively seeking out alternative viewpoints can stave off conformist thinking and mitigate decision-making risks.

Actively listening and elevating employee voices is also about responding genuinely and proactively. Feedback, ideas, or concerns should not disappear into a black hole but should lead to visible changes—helping employees feel seen, heard, and appreciated. This authentic action strongly validates the importance you place on their voice.

Ultimately, it's not about doing all the talking or engaging in monologues—it's about dialing up the dialogue and turning down the decibels of top-down management. It's about creating an environment that thrives on synergy and collaboration—an environment where everyone's voice echoes equally.

In conclusion, elevating employee voices through active listening is not just beneficial—it's essential. By embracing this attitude in your daily interactions, you'll soon see a transformative shift in your leadership style and organization's overall dynamics. After all, when every person feels valued, heard, and understood at work—they naturally strive harder, innovate more creatively, and stick around longer—all contributing to a more competitive business in today's fast-paced world.

Case Studies: The Transformative Power of Leaders who Prioritize Listening

In a world where leaders often communicate more than they listen, the ones who prioritize listening stand out. Through case studies and examples, we shall underscore the transformative power of such individuals—the iconic leaders who make a conscious effort to understand their teams through active listening.

The story of Satya Nadella, CEO of Microsoft, serves as an illustrative example. Upon assuming office in 2014, Nadella embarked on a listening tour across the globe, meeting with employees from all levels of the organization. He invited their opinions and perspectives and demonstrated consistent empathy—attributes central to the practice of *iconic listening*. Under his leadership, Microsoft saw not just significant financial growth but also critical improvements in employee satisfaction and company culture.

The second case study is that of Mary Barra, the CEO of General Motors. Recognized as one of the world's most powerful women, her emphasis on listening has played a crucial role in shaping her leadership style. Barra regularly hosts town halls and round-table discussions with staff members at all levels to understand their experiences better. She's noted saying, "When you really listen to someone—and show them you're listening—they're more likely to put forth their best ideas."

These two examples highlight an important aspect—**transformative power of leaders who prioritize listening**. By taking time to truly understand their employees' perspectives, both Nadella and Barra have succeeded in inspiring trust among their workforce, fostering an environment conducive for innovation.

In today's job market characterized by numerous options for employees, companies are recognizing this practice's value in retaining talent. Whether it's tech giant Google or retail powerhouse Nordstrom, companies consistently ranked 'best places to work' often have one thing in common—recognition of the strength that employee voices bring to the table.

It's important to note that these case studies are not exceptions. Rather, they're a part of an **increasing trend where active listening is being recognized as a key leadership trait.** According to a Harvard Business Review study, leaders who listen well are more likely to inspire higher levels of trust and employee engagement.

In conclusion, the transformational impact of prioritizing listening is profound. Leaders who master this skill can expect not just an engaged and innovative workforce but also improvements in overall organizational performance. Perhaps it's time we shift our focus from asking leaders to 'talk the talk' and urge them to 'listen the listen', instead.

Focusing on Prioritizing Listening in Leadership

When building a successful leadership style, it is essential to prioritize listening. However, most people may wonder, how do you place listening at the forefront of your communication strategy? Let us delve into how leaders can truly make a shift towards prioritizing listening in leadership.

Firstly, for leaders to prioritize listening, they need to create and cultivate an environment that fosters open communication. This could be done by implementing regular check-ins with team members, where leaders genuinely focus on what the employees have to say rather than dominating the conversation. It's not just about giving orders or delegating tasks, but also actively seeking input from team members about decisions and actions.

Prioritizing listening also means paying attention not only to verbal cues but also non-verbal ones. Often, what isn't spoken carries a wealth of information. An employee's body language, tone of voice or even their silences can speak volumes about their feelings and perspectives if interpreted correctly.

Prioritizing active listening in leadership also involves being fully present during conversations. As a leader, it's easy to get overwhelmed with multitasking – responding to emails, attending meetings or strategizing next steps – while having conversations with team members. However, active listening requires full attention in order to truly understand and engage with what's being communicated.

Leaders should not just listen for the sake of appearing like good listeners; they must demonstrate genuine eagerness and curiosity in understanding their employees' viewpoints. This means asking clarifying questions when necessary and paraphrasing the speaker's main points to confirm understanding. In this way, they show their respect for others by putting themselves in their shoes and trying to see issues from their perspective.

A crucial part of prioritizing listening in leadership is responding promptly. Listening isn't simply about being a sounding board for problems; leaders need to take swift and appropriate action based on the feedback received. This shows employees that not only their voices are heard, but also they are considered valuable and significant in the decision-making process.

Furthermore, it's important for leaders to encourage open and honest feedback from their team by making it safe to voice dissenting opinions or concerns. Effective listening involves acknowledging these different perspectives without judgment, fostering a culture of openness and respect.

Lastly, when focusing on prioritizing listening in your leadership style, remember that this is an ongoing process. It requires constant effort, practice and self-awareness to avoid falling into the trap of 'pretend listening' where you appear to listen but your mind is elsewhere.

In conclusion, prioritizing listening in leadership is crucial for building stronger relationships with your team members, encouraging creativity and innovation and fostering an environment of trust. Leaders who successfully prioritize listening can benefit from improved team dynamics, higher employee engagement levels and ultimately a more efficient and productive workforce. Remember - it's not always about the loudest voice; sometimes, it's the quietest voice which has the most impactful things to say!

XI. Iconic Decision-Making: Balancing Boldness and Pragmatism

In the realm of business and corporate leadership, few things are as crucial or transformational as visionary decision-making. The ability to look beyond the confines of the present, perceive potential future trajectories, and make strategic decisions that drive an organization forward is what sets iconic leaders apart. This ability forms the foundation of what we often refer to as an *'iconic leadership legacy'*.

A truly visionary leader is more than just a strategist or a decision-maker. They are decisive in their actions, bold in their choices, and dauntless in their outlook. But what does it mean to be a *'decisive and visionary leader'*? How does one balance practical considerations with bold initiatives? And most importantly, how can such leadership shape an unforgettable legacy?

Decisive and visionary leaders are characterized by their ability to take calculated risks, think outside the box, and foresee trends before they become apparent. Yet beyond that, they are also defined by their unwavering commitment to their team and their vision for the organization.

In our rapidly changing world, where uncertainties abound, the importance of visionary leadership cannot be overstated. Amidst all the chaos and ambiguity, organizations look up to leaders who can provide direction, chart out a clear path, and inspire confidence amongst their ranks. This is where decisive decision-making plays a vital role.

Decisive decision-making is not about making quick and hasty decisions. Instead, it refers to leaders' ability to make informed choices confidently after considering all relevant factors. These decisions, made in moments of crisis or stability alike, can significantly impact the course of the organization's journey. When combined with a visionary outlook, this form of decision-making powerfully shapes an organization, leaving behind a mark - an *'iconic leadership legacy'*.

However, the journey from being a leader to leaving behind a legacy is complex and multifaceted. It demands not only visionary decision-making but also values-driven actions, bold initiatives, empathy towards team members, constant learning, and adaptation to changing scenarios. This multidimensional journey of leadership forms the crux of our discussion.

In this comprehensive section, we will dive deeper into understanding the role of decisive and visionary decision-making in shaping an iconic leadership legacy. We will also explore how balancing bold initiatives with practical considerations can ensure sustainable success for leaders and their organizations.

Through real-world examples, case studies, and insights from renowned leaders, we aim to provide a clear roadmap for those aspiring to transform their leadership style and leave behind a distinguished legacy. So, let's embark on this journey of leadership transformation together.

Incorporating Values and Bold Initiatives in Leadership Vision

While the foundation of an iconic leadership legacy lies in visionary and decisive decision-making, the blueprint includes much more. One such vital component is incorporating values and undertaking bold initiatives. These are not only integral parts of a leader's vision but also pivotal indicators of their capability to steer their team towards leadership success.

In the journey towards establishing an iconic leadership legacy, charting out and acting upon bold ideas is an invaluable attribute. Bold initiatives signify a leader's courage to challenge conventional norms, disrupt traditional business models, and strive for innovation. However, these initiatives should resonate with the core values of both the organization and its people – making this a complex yet crucial aspect of transformative leadership.

A striking example would be Steve Jobs' launch of the iPhone in 2007. This was indeed a bold initiative that represented Jobs' confidence to challenge industry norms by introducing a revolutionized communication device. His decision derived from Apple's core value: "Think Different". Despite skepticism and criticism, Jobs stuck firmly to his decision, convinced about his forward-looking vision. The result? iPhone became one of the most successful consumer electronics products ever created, shaping Jobs' legacy as an iconic visionary leader who dared to go where no one had gone before.

A similar example can be gleaned from Elon Musk's journey where he undertook multiple bold initiatives guided by his personal ethos and Tesla Inc.'s shared values. From launching electric vehicles at scale when critics deemed them unviable, to conceptualizing Hyperloop when faster land transport seemed like a far-off dream - Musk's leadership portrayed nothing short of relentless dedication towards achieving sustainable mobility.

From these instances it becomes clear that daring to take bold decisions does not always promise immediate victory. Rather, it often invites cynicism and resistance. Yet, it is these audacious moves that truly characterize visionary leaders.

Nonetheless, what sets successful leaders apart is their steadfast commitment to their vision even while facing adversity. They understand that making a bold decision is just the first step - they need to follow it up with unwavering effort, indomitable conviction, and the ability to align their team's efforts with their daring goal. This alignment plays a significant role in translating the bold envisage into actionable strategies and processes that lead towards sustainable success.

In this context, an emerging leadership model, called "Values-based Leadership", holds immense relevance. This framework emphasizes the importance of aligning bold initiatives with the fundamental values of an organization – ensuring not only strategic direction but also fostering unity and commitment among team members.

A Values-based Leader recognizes that bold decisions guided by core values drive positive culture, fosters trust within the organization, encourages innovative thinking, and contributes towards team morale – all of which are vital for creating a lasting leadership legacy.

In conclusion, incorporating values and undertaking bold initiatives in leadership vision can significantly contribute to shaping an iconic leadership legacy. It exemplifies courage and an unwavering belief in a better future, making such leaders sources of inspiration for others. As we move forward into discussing the balance between visionary thoughts and practical considerations, remember that every great initiative begins with a bold yet value-driven decision.

Balancing Leadership Vision with Practical Considerations

Navigating the thin line between visionary leadership and practical realities is a challenge that every leader faces. To execute bold initiatives effectively and drive organization towards sustainable success, balancing visionary thoughts with practical considerations becomes an indispensable aspect of decision-making.

Having a grand vision is undoubtedly crucial for iconic leadership but a vision without consideration of its applicability in real-world scenarios can prove detrimental to the organization. One may have groundbreaking ideas but translating them into reality demands awareness about existing resources, constraints, market trends, potential risks, and team capabilities.

Take the example of Jeff Bezos who dreamed of creating the world's most customer-centric company: Amazon. His vision was undeniably giant-size - "to sell everything to everyone everywhere in the world," yet his approach towards achieving it was step by step and very practical. From starting as an online bookstore to gradually expanding its product categories over many years – Bezos' decisions were strategic, well-timed, and aligned with market readiness and internal resources.

This case exemplifies that even when pursuing a bold vision, leaders need to embrace practical wisdom. They need to adapt their strategies according to ever-changing external environments and internal dynamics and make informed decisions based on data, insights and feedback.

Practical considerations also involve understanding your team's abilities. A leader should gauge whether their team possesses the required skills or needs training for certain tasks. After all, successful execution of any plan greatly depends on how efficiently a team can implement it.

In addition, leaders must also consider financial realities. Imprudent financial decisions made in pursuit of hasty growth can lead to catastrophic consequences for an organisation's sustainability. Finding ways to fund your operations while ensuring minimal debts is a necessary part of realistic planning.

A visionary approach and decisiveness in decision-making cannot overlook these practical considerations if the vision is to be turned into reality. Balancing the two might require making some tough calls – you might need to revise your timelines, scale down or pivot your plans, or rethink resources allocation. Yet what matters in the end is achieving long-term success without compromising organizational stability.

Leaders who can successfully strike a balance between their expansive vision and practicalities foster teams that are both motivated and realistic about their goals. Such leaders inspire confidence because they demonstrate that while they dream big, they also have a pragmatic plan to achieve those dreams.

To conclude, visionary leadership is not just about having ambitious ideas and making bold decisions—it also involves understanding the limitations of current circumstances and effectively maneuvering around them. Visionary leaders who make space for practical considerations in their thought process stand at a higher likelihood of leaving behind an iconic leadership legacy. As we delve deeper into this subject, we'll next explore how visionary decision-making significantly impacts team morale.

The Impact of Visionary Decision-Making on Team Morale

Leadership is not just about making big decisions or carrying out bold initiatives. Another essential aspect of leadership involves bearing the responsibility for your team's morale. In this section, we'll delve into the critical role that visionary decision-making plays in shaping team morale and how it subsequently influences an organization's success.

Visionary leaders understand that their company's greatest asset isn't a unique business model or ground-breaking technology – it's their people. They recognize that their decisions impact not only their team members' performance but also their motivation, commitment, and job satisfaction.

An effective leader recognizes that participatory decision-making can strengthen trust between them and their teams. When they allow others to contribute to critical decisions, they empower them. This sense of empowerment adds to the team morale and encourages employees to take ownership of their tasks, leading to increased productivity and dedication.

A case in point is Satya Nadella's transformative leadership at Microsoft. Nadella placed significant emphasis on changing the company culture and boosting employee morale. His vision was centered around 'empowering every person and every organization on the planet to achieve more'. And he put these words into action by fostering a culture of inclusivity, collaboration, and growth mindset - ensuring his visionary decision-making incorporated his team's voice.

Such participative decision-making reflects a leader's trust in their team's skills and abilities, which significantly enhances team morale. High team morale often translates into high team performance - resulting in improved efficiency, lower turnover rates, and overall organizational success.

Team impact is two-fold when it comes to visionary decision-making. On one hand, a leader's decisions affect the course the team takes; on the other hand, a motivated and enthusiastic team can influence the quality of those decisions. Mutual trust, open communication, and a participatory environment for decision-making create a positive feedback loop that enhances both leadership and team morale.

Additionally, visionary leaders acknowledge and prioritize their teams' wellbeing and job satisfaction. They invest time to understand their team members' aspirations and challenges, making decisions that foster personal growth alongside organizational progress. This recognition and understanding contribute towards an enriched work culture where employees feel valued - significantly amplifying team morale.

Another approach used by visionary leaders to boost morale is through transparent communication about their decisions' rationale. When a leader openly shares their thought process behind critical decisions, it eliminates ambiguity and anxiety within the team. Transparency fosters trust, engenders respect, and boosts team morale.

To conclude this section, the impact of visionary decision-making on team morale cannot be dismissed. Leaders who attain a balance of keeping their eyes on the horizon while staying grounded in their teams' realities lay down a foundation of high morale within their organization. Such boosted morale is not only instrumental in day-to-day operations but also positively impacts long-term outcomes. With this understanding in place, let's move forward to explore how lessons learned from past decision points can sculpt your future course.

Lessons learned from past decision points & their future implications

As we traverse the leadership journey, it is inevitable to come across turning points or critical decision-making junctures - moments that hold immense power in shaping a leader's path. These critical decision points not only bear significant consequences but often come packed with precious learning opportunities. This section will delve into understanding how lessons drawn from such crucial junctures can influence the course of a visionary leader's journey and impact their team's morale.

The business landscape is fraught with instances where leaders have faced significant crossroads - be it a challenging market downturn, an organizational crisis, or even a global pandemic. Visionary leaders do not view these scenarios merely as obstacles; instead, they see them as stepping stones towards learning, growth, and innovation. They understand that *'lessons learned'* from these critical decisions can provide valuable insights for future strategy formulation and implementation.

A notable example would be the leadership journey of Reed Hastings, the founder of Netflix. At a time when Blockbuster was dominating video rentals, Netflix faced significant difficulties in scaling its DVD-by-mail service. However, rather than merely copying industry norms or giving up, Hastings took a bold step forward - he envisioned on-demand streaming services at a time when the idea seemed far-fetched. The result? Today Netflix is among the leading entertainment platforms globally and Hastings' visionary leadership has been instrumental to this success.

However, the massive success did not come without trials and errors. Netflix encountered several stumbling blocks throughout its evolution - including a substantial backlash against its Qwikster spin-off plan in 2011 which intended to separate DVD rental and streaming services into two different websites. Recognizing customer dissatisfaction, Hastings quickly reverted the decision - demonstrating humility and adaptability in recognizing mistakes and making amends.

The Netflix story is a testament to how visionary leaders can learn from their decision points, even those leading to missteps, and use these lessons for future improvements. Leaders who acknowledge their mistakes and take corrective action not only find better solutions but also gain respect from their teams - boosting morale and fostering an open culture that values feedback and learning.

Leadership, much like any other journey, involves its share of trials, errors, successes, and failures. Visionary leaders recognize this aspect and incorporate it into their leadership approach. They understand that every decision they make serves as a learning opportunity that could potentially shape the next big step or transformation in their organization's journey towards sustainable success.

In essence, each crucial decision point – whether resulting in success or failure – offers valuable lessons which serve as guiding lights for future pathways. By embracing these lessons with an open mind and heart, leaders can navigate through complexities with heightened wisdom, leading to improved decision-making capability over time. This continuous learning cycle not only enhances the leader's own abilities but also imbues the entire team with a growth mindset - positively impacting team morale.

Hence, the impact of past decision points goes beyond just immediate outcomes; they hold the power to shape future leadership actions and influence ongoing team spirit. In the upcoming section, we will further expand on how such accumulative experiences contribute to shaping a sustainable leadership legacy.

Chapter **10**

Boosting Team Motivation & Productivity: Creating Meaningful Rituals for Employee Recognition

In today's competitive business landscape, a key driver of organizational success lies in the hands of its workforce. Recognizing and appreciating the hard work of employees can often be the catalyst not just for individual motivation, but also collective productivity within teams. This invaluable strategy of employee recognition has proven to play a pivotal role in fostering a workplace where team members feel valued and integral to the organization.

So why is employee recognition such a crucial aspect for businesses? Consider this: A study indicates that 68% of employees say that recognition is the top motivator for performance improvement. When employees are acknowledged for their individual efforts, they experience an increased sense of worth, leading to greater job satisfaction and more heightened performance levels.

Forecasting the long-term benefits, consistent recognition in the form of public praise, certificates, or even employee appreciation quotes can significantly influence employee retention rates. People are more likely to stay with an organization where their hard work is recognized and rewarded. Furthermore, it positively affects employee morale, as appreciation from managers inspires employees to work harder and stay loyal to their organization.

Acknowledgement fuels what can be termed as the 'ripple effect' on team motivation. Just as a stone tossed into a pond creates ripples, consistent appreciation impacts not just the receiver but also other team members who observe this act. They too are motivated to achieve their goals and contribute constructively towards the well-being of the organization.

This ripple effect doesn't stop at team motivation – it also positively impacts productivity. Continuous recognition provides a sense of achievement, empowering employees to strive for excellence and deliver better results. Moreover, when team members recognize each other's' achievements, it nurtures a collaborative and supportive environment, further enhancing overall productivity.

Yet, for these results to materialize, it is essential that recognition is personalized and meaningful. Generic or insincere appreciation can do more harm than good. This is where personalized recognition strategies come into play - a topic we will delve into in the next section of this book.

In conclusion, recognizing and celebrating achievements sends a clear message to employees: their hard work matters. In doing so, it fosters an environment where every team member feels valued, thereby boosting motivation and productivity. Remember, a simple act of gratitude can create a ripple effect that uplifts your entire workforce.

Now that we've established the pivotal role recognition plays within an organization, let's move on to discuss one such strategy – creating meaningful rituals – and how they enhance both individual fulfilment and collective success at the workplace. Stay tuned!

The Concept of Meaningful Rituals in the Workplace

While some may associate the word 'ritual' with religious or cultural ceremonies, when it comes to the workplace, rituals take on a different connotation. In this context, a ritual is a routine or habit that has more significant symbolic meaning – something repetitive, yet with profound emotional engagement.

In essence, meaningful rituals at work involve acknowledging and celebrating achievements – be they large-scale team successes or individual milestones. Going beyond mere high fives and pats on the back, these rituals can create lasting impact, fostering a culture where each employee feels seen, heard, and recognised for their unique contributions.

These managed moments within an organization can be as diverse as the workforce itself. For instance, one company might have monthly award ceremonies celebrating outstanding performers. A different business might provide a platform for employees to share their personal 'wins' at weekly team meetings. Other workplaces might recognize accomplishments through newsletters distributed internally or special mentions during town hall meetings.

Rituals play an essential role in building the identity of an organization - they're not just about rewarding success but also about reiterating the beliefs and values upon which a business stands. These repeated actions mirror what the company values – whether it's innovation, teamwork, integrity or high-performance.

Acknowledging every team achievement, even those seemingly small victories, fosters positive reinforcement among team members. This act of acknowledgment creates an environment where employees know their efforts matter and are not going unnoticed. Accomplishments need not always be work-related; celebrating personal wins such as anniversaries or birthdays can also contribute to making employees feel appreciated and valued.

Meaningful rituals vary from organization to organization - there's no one-size-fits-all. These could range from team lunches for completing a successful project, to employees ringing a bell for closed deals, or even showcasing employee appreciation messages on the company's social media platforms or internal communications board.

To make these rituals meaningful, their personalization is paramount. Personalized recognition makes these moments more authentic and resonant. Employees enjoy being recognized in unique ways that speak to their contributions and character. It nurtures a sense of belonging and promotes emotional connections with their peers and the organization at large.

In a nutshell, meaningful workplace rituals contribute significantly by recognizing and valuing the efforts of all employees. They play an indispensable part in fostering a positive work environment where everyone feels involved, appreciated, and motivated to perform better. The key lies in creating rituals that resonate with your workforce's uniqueness - making them feel integral to the overall scheme of things within your organization.

Tune in for our next section where we'll delve into various personalized recognition strategies that you can implement to create these meaningful experiences for your workforce.

Implementing Personalized Recognition Strategies

Having established the importance of meaningful rituals in creating an environment where employees feel valued and integral, it is crucial to understand that recognizing their individuality paves the way for a more engaged workforce. That's where personalized recognition strategies enter the picture, providing a tailored approach to appreciating and rewarding employees for their contributions.

Personalization in employee recognition isn't merely about attaching names to achievements; it is about genuinely understanding what each employee values and appreciates — thereby making recognition an even more powerful motivator. This involves considering factors such as the employee's role, their preferences for private or public acknowledgment, or even matching the type of recognition to their unique contribution.

Recognizing achievements, major or minor, should be aligned with what the individual values most. For instance, some employees would appreciate a public announcement celebrating their accomplishment at a team meeting while others may prefer a personal note from the management. It could also involve creative gestures like personalised 'thank you' notes or unique tokens of appreciation.

If your organization has diverse teams spread across various locations, leverage technology to bridge the gap. Digital platforms that enable peer-to-peer or managerial recognitions are highly effective in today's virtual work culture. These can range from virtual "high-fives" on communication platforms or featuring accomplishments on company webpages and social media.

The key is to ensure that recognition strategies are regularly revisited and adjusted as per employee feedbacks and changing dynamics. In fact, involving employees in crafting these strategies could be a powerful way of ensuring they resonate effectively.

A great example of personalized recognition comes from Salesforce. They use a unique platform called Work.com to encourage real-time acknowledgement amongst coworkers. The system allows peers to give each other 'badges' for their achievements—these badges not only recognize an employee's contributions but are also tied to the company values, thereby aligning individual efforts with organizational objectives.

Another creative approach is adopted by Google, where managers can distribute 'kudos' or 'peer bonuses.' Employees get to choose from a variety of rewards best suited to them - from personal training sessions to cooking classes - ensuring recognition is highly personalized and appreciated by recipients.

In essence, personalized recognition strategies encapsulate the premise that valuing employees isn't a one-size-fits-all proposition. It requires thoughtful planning and execution to ensure it strikes the right chord with every individual. By doing so, you foster an environment where each member feels acknowledged for his unique input, enhancing their sense of belonging and motivation towards their work, thereby significantly impacting overall team morale and productivity.

In our subsequent section, we'll explore how empowering your workforce complements these recognition strategies, creating a harmonious ecosystem that encourages each individual's optimum contribution to the organization. Stay tuned!

Reinforcing Employee Recognition with Empowerment

Recognizing and appreciating employees for their contributions is a fantastic way to make them feel valued and integral. However, this alone is not enough. To truly cultivate an environment where individuals are motivated and productive, they must also be empowered. This means entrusting them with responsibilities, providing them the freedom to perform tasks in their own unique ways, and supporting them in their growth.

Employee empowerment stands as a cornerstone in the foundation of any successful organization. It's about enabling individuals to utilize their potential fully, equipping them with the skills, resources, opportunity and motivation necessary to accomplish their work-related responsibilities effectively.

This approach is particularly effective because it aligns neatly with the concept of recognition. As we empower our employees by investing in their development —through training programs, regular feedback sessions or opportunities for professional advancement— we're inherently recognizing their value and potential contribution to the organization.

In essence, employee empowerment serves as an extension of recognition strategies. By providing your team members with the tools they need to succeed, you're acknowledging their capabilities while encouraging performance improvement.

An empowered workforce leads to enhanced job satisfaction and better results; when workers feel they have control over how they carry out their duties, they are more likely to take ownership of their work and strive for improved outcomes. The result is a positive cycle where productivity boosts overall employee morale, which in turn further drives productivity.

A business that fosters this type of environment showcases its commitment towards fostering an environment conducive to individual growth — thereby making team motivation not just aspirational but achievable.

The notion of empowering employees should go beyond the immediate workplace scenario; it should promote a culture of learning where individuals are encouraged to broaden their horizons. Google's '20 percent time' policy is a great example of this approach. It encourages employees to spend 20% of their working time on individual projects that interest them, leading not just to enhanced skills but also groundbreaking innovations.

At the core of it all is giving employees a voice—listening and responding to their expectations and concerns. Encourage open communication where people are free to express ideas, feedback or issues without fear of judgement.

Remember - an empowered employee is an engaged employee, and an engaged employee is a productive one. When you recognise your workers, make sure you're also empowering them in equal measure. This balance will set the stage for a motivated, satisfied workforce, ready to achieve both personal growth and organisational success.

Up next, we'll explore how recognition can be utilized as an effective tool for enhancing team motivation and productivity. Read on!

Utilizing Recognition as a Tool for Enhancing Team Motivation and Productivity

In the preceding sections, we have discussed the significance of employee recognition and empowerment in fostering a culture of appreciation. Now, let's dive deep into how recognition serves as an impactful tool to boost team motivation and overall productivity.

Motivation is the driving force that influences employees' attitudes, behavior, satisfaction, and performance levels. When a team member feels appreciated for their efforts, it injects new energy and motivation to strive harder. They feel a sense of belonging with stronger engagement towards their organization which creates a ripple effect on overall team spirit and productivity.

Businesses can take several routes to integrate recognition strategies that enhance team motivation; these may include public praise, financial incentives, promotions or opportunities for personal development such as training programs or conferences.

The key here is to ensure the form of acknowledgement matches the achievement. For instance, acknowledging a significant project success might involve a thoughtful reward or bonus scheme whereas celebrating everyday wins could be presented through simple gestures like sharing employee appreciation quotes.

Beyond individual accomplishments, appreciating team achievements fosters unity, cooperation and better communication among peers. This builds a shared sense of purpose where everyone strives together towards common goals thus leading to enhanced team productivity.

A study conducted by the Society for Human Resource Management (SHRM) reveals that recognition has a strong influence on employee engagement levels - which directly impacts productivity. The findings indicated that employees who are recognized are more likely to rate their workplace as engaging which boosts their morale and enhances their functioning capacities.

An example practice involves leveraging technology through platforms like Slack or Microsoft Teams to celebrate successes via virtual high-fives or shout-outs. Not only does this provide instant recognition, but it also makes the process transparent and encourages others to join in the appreciation, thereby boosting morale and motivation.

Apart from digital platforms, traditional methods of recognition like an appreciative email or a handwritten note still hold potent value. Personal forms of recognition like these have a deep impact on an employee's psyche, making them feel valued and integral – subsequently driving their motivation.

Remember that motivation is a crucial ingredient for ensuring high productivity levels. A motivated workforce proactively seeks ways to improve performance and contribute towards business objectives. Ultimately, recognizing employees' hard work creates an environment that enables your workforce to feel encouraged to keep moving forward, increasing job satisfaction while enhancing overall productivity levels.

Chapter 11

Iconic Mentorship: Cultivating the Next Generation of Leaders

In the realm of organizational growth and personal development, two terms frequently surface in contemporary discourse: iconic leadership and empowering mentorship. While they may seem distinct, these two concepts are closely linked and often serve as catalysts for individual growth and organizational process enhancement.

What is Iconic Leadership?

Iconic leadership is a form of transformative influence that transcends conventional notions of authority and management. An iconic leader is not merely an individual who stands at the helm of an organization or leads a team. They are exceptional visionaries, whose remarkable insights and innovative actions create a significant ripple effect within their respective spheres of influence. They craft a legacy that contributes to shaping cultures, industries, and societies at large.

The Essence of Empowering Mentorship

If iconic leadership is the beacon guiding the path towards progress, empowering mentorship is the vessel that facilitates this journey for emerging leaders. Empowering mentorship is centered around inspiring confidence, fostering autonomy, nurturing talents, and capacitating individuals to reach their full potential. It allows for the mentee to take driving seat under the guidance and supervision of the mentor.

Mentorship that empowers not only imparts knowledge and skills but also fosters a sense of self-belief, autonomy, and resilience in mentees. Its essence lies in the transition from being directed to becoming self-directed—taking charge of one's destiny while navigating life tools gleaned from a mentor.

The Symbiosis of Iconic Leadership and Empowering Mentorship

At first glance, it seems like iconic leadership and empowering mentorship exist in separate silos—one dealing with individuals influencing masses while the other focusing on a one-on-one relationship. However, in reality, these two principles are intrinsically intertwined and are often the gears in the machinery of success within a thriving organization or community.

An iconic leader is likely to be an excellent mentor due to their experience, insights, and innovative mindset. Conversely, an empowering mentor can cultivate future iconic leaders by instilling confidence and self-belief, providing guidance, and nurturing talents. The relationship between an iconic leader and a mentee fosters a conducive environment for personal and professional growth. This relationship further stimulates creativity, incites innovation, and drives organizational change.

In conclusion, iconic leadership and empowering mentorship are not just about taking charge and leading others or about passing on wisdom and knowledge to mentees. It's about creating a transformative influence that reshapes the landscape of organizations and societies. These concepts target the holistic development of individuals—their knowledge, skills, perspective—and contribute towards creating a more dynamic, inclusive, and innovative work environment.

The Impact of an Iconic Leader on the Mentorship Landscape

Iconic leaders have been known to leave a significant impact on the mentorship landscape. Their uniquely innovative approaches to leadership, grounded in empathy, vision and courage, often bring a refreshing perspective towards nurturing talent within organizations.

A New Era of Leadership

As we further delve into the impact that iconic leaders have on mentorship, it becomes evident that they are not merely guides for their mentees but pioneers in creating new paradigms of leadership. Transformative leaders break free from conventional methods and practices. They embrace forward-thinking strategies and create unique paths toward success. This innovation in approach is not confined to their direct sphere of influence but spreads to the broader mentorship landscape, revolutionizing traditional perspectives on leadership and guidance.

The Reshaping of The Mentor-Mentee Relationship

The profound influence of these iconic leaders also reshapes the dynamics of the mentor-mentee relationship. No longer is this relationship perceived as a one-way flow of knowledge and instruction from the mentor to mentee. Instead, guided by an iconic leader, this bond evolves into a symbiotic partnership where both parties learn, grow, inspire and challenge each other. Through their actions and words, iconic leaders demonstrate that mentoring isn't about moulding mentees in their own image; rather, it's about allowing them space to shape and discover their own path.

Influence on Organizational Culture and Values

Furthermore, iconic leaders can significantly influence organizational culture and values through their mentorship endeavors. By fostering an environment of continuous learning, respect for individuality, tolerance for mistakes, and encouragement for innovation - they help instill strong work ethics rooted in humanistic values. Their reach extends beyond individual mentees - permeating throughout the organization, inspiring a culture of mentorship that encourages employees at all levels to learn from and support one another.

The Creation of a Ripple Effect

Lastly, the transformative influence of an iconic leader in the field of mentorship doesn't stop within their immediate surroundings or organizations. Their progressive ideas often create a ripple effect, carrying far-reaching implications for the larger professional and business community. Empowered by such leaders' visionary strategies, many mentees emerge as future leaders themselves, carrying forth this legacy of enlightened, transformative leadership. This ripple effect helps create a positive shift in the general landscape of mentorship, making it more dynamic, inclusive and empowering for everyone involved.

In essence, the impact of iconic leaders on the mentorship landscape isn't confined to merely guiding individuals or shaping organizational cultures. These leaders inspire revolutionary changes that reorient traditional notions about leadership and mentoring - making way for a construct that is more balanced, holistic and meaningful in today's increasingly complex and diverse world.

Transformative Influence of an Iconic Leader

The transformative influence of an iconic leader is often seen as a game-changer in various spheres of life and work. Their impact can range from altering the cultural dynamics within their organizations to sparking industry-wide shifts and revolutions. The heart of this transformative influence lies in two things: vision incubation and execution.

The Vision Incubation

Iconic leaders are known for having a compelling vision — one that's not just focused on short-term goals, but which also considers the broader picture regarding society, industry, and future generations. This vision serves as the foundation for their leadership style, inspiring others around them to believe in it and strive to make it a reality.

The Execution

The second aspect of their transformative influence involves the implementation or execution of this vision. Iconic leaders are not just dreamers; they convert their visions into attainable strategies by leading through example and exhibiting determination, resilience, and adaptability. They set themselves apart by successfully translating innovative ideas into successful businesses, community movements, or industry trends.

Real-life Case Studies

Examining real-life instances can further illustrate the transformative influence of iconic leaders. A stark example of such leadership can be seen in Steve Jobs, co-founder of Apple Inc. His initial vision revolved around making computers accessible to everyday consumers rather than just businesses or institutes. Despite various setbacks, he persisted with his vision, ultimately revolutionizing personal computing, music distribution, and mobile technology industries.

Subtle Shifts

Still, transformations brought about by iconic leaders are not always grandiose or immediately visible; sometimes they involve subtle shifts over time that significantly alter the course of events. Consider Indra Nooyi's tenure as CEO of PepsiCo. She transformed the company by steering it towards more health-conscious products and sustainability efforts, despite initial resistance. Her influence led to a shift in the corporate landscape, encouraging businesses worldwide to consider their environmental impact and consumer health.

Seismic Shifts

In contrast, some iconic leaders catalyze seismic shifts and sudden revolutions. Take Elon Musk for instance; his ambitious vision of a sustainable future and disruptive innovations in electric vehicles (Tesla) and space exploration (SpaceX) are challenging norms across multiple industries. His transformative leadership is not only pushing boundaries but is also inspiring a new generation of innovators and entrepreneurs.

Overall, iconic leaders have one thing in common — they instigate change. This change could be experienced within an individual, a team, an organization, or even across nations and generations. Their courage to steer away from the status quo, combined with their visionary thinking and ability to execute ideas effectively, makes their influence truly transformative.

Strategies for Nurturing and Empowering Emerging Leaders Within the Organization

The role of nurturing future leadership within an organization cannot be overstated. Having a pool of competent, empowered leaders at various levels not only ensures smooth succession planning but also promotes a culture of innovation, effectiveness and resilience. Here are some crucial strategies used by successful organizations to nurture and empower emerging leaders.

Targeted Development Programs

Targeted development programs account for a significant part of leadership cultivation efforts. These may include on-the-job experiences, coaching sessions, workshops, or formal training programs which aim at developing requisite leadership skills among prospective leaders. For example, Google's "Project Oxygen" was about arming managers with necessary management tools – from providing constructive feedback to empowering teams.

Creating Leadership Opportunities

Rather than waiting for traditional leadership roles to open up, progressive organizations create leadership opportunities at various levels. Providing potential leaders with responsibilities beyond their standard job functions allows them to develop and display their leadership abilities. This could be in the form of leading a project team, heading a committee or task force, or managing an important initiative.

Embracing Risk-Taking

Emerging leaders must feel safe to take risks and make decisions that they believe in. Organizations can nurture this behavior by promoting a culture where failure is viewed as a part of learning rather than as an end result. This encourages employees to step out of their comfort zones and fosters creativity and innovation.

Mentorship

Mentorship is pivotal in fostering emerging leaders. Mentors offer valuable insights based on their experience and often act as sounding boards for new ideas. They also play key roles in shaping values, instilling confidence, providing networking opportunities and preparing future leaders for challenges. The mentor-mentee relationship often goes beyond professional development, encompassing personal growth as well.

Feedback and Recognition

Providing constructive feedback and recognizing efforts is fundamental in nurturing emerging leaders. Regularly assessing performance and offering praise and recognition when deserved helps employees understand where they stand. It also motivates them to improve, helping them realize their potential within the organization.

Inclusive Leadership Programs

Successful organizations focus on incorporating diversity and inclusivity within their leadership. This includes recruitment from diverse backgrounds and fostering a culture that respects different views and experiences. Such an environment promotes the exchange of creative ideas, encourages healthy discussions, reducing biases, competition, and promoting collective success.

To sum up, nurturing emerging leaders is a continuous process demanding commitment and strategic planning by the organization. By focusing on these strategies, organizations can reap benefits like increased productivity, improved retention rates, enhanced innovation and ultimately a more resilient organization able to take on future challenges with confidence.

Spotlight on Successful Mentees

In the palette of success, mentees turned leaders colour some of the brightest and most inspiring stories. Beneath the broad strokes of their achievements often lies a myriad of nurturing relationships and empowering guidance from iconic mentors. To further grasp this phenomenon, let's turn our attention to some examples.

The Road to Becoming a Visionary Leader

Sherly Sandberg, an iconic leader herself now, was once mentored by another inspiring individual - her professor, Larry Summers. During her time at Harvard, Summers took notice of Sandberg's potential and took her under his wing. They maintained their mentor-mentee relationship even as they climbed career ladders; firstly at World Bank, later at Google and finally at Facebook where she now serves as the Chief Operating Officer.

Sandberg credits Summers for his profound influence on her leadership style. His unshakable belief in her potential not only bolstered her confidence but also shaped her philosophy on leadership—urging others to "lean in." Sherly Sandberg's growth trajectory attests to how mentorship can empower individuals to conquer self-doubt, break glass ceilings and emerge as visionary leaders themselves.

Mentoring Fuels Innovation

Another inspiring example includes that of Mark Zuckerberg and Steve Jobs. Jobs was never an official mentor to Zuckerberg; however, he played a pivotal role in shaping Zuckerberg's approach to business and innovation. This informal mentorship started when Facebook was still a growing company. Whenever Zuckerberg faced difficulties or uncertainties regarding Facebook's future direction, Jobs would provide invaluable advice drawn from his own experiences.

Jobs encouraged Zuckerberg to focus more on building high-quality products instead of getting driven by quick profits—an advice that evidently influenced Facebook's strategy over the years. The exchange of ideas between these two pioneers highlights how mentorship can fuel innovation, even when it transcends traditional structures.

Mentorship Encourages Social Change

Moving beyond the corporate world, let's look at Nobel Peace Prize laureate Malala Yousafzai. Her father Ziauddin Yousafzai was an educator and a strong advocate for girls' education in Pakistan—a belief that clearly influenced Malala. Despite facing threats from extremist groups, he encouraged Malala to continue her education and stand up for her rights. His mentorship not only fostered courage in Malala but also empowered her to become a global spokesperson for girls' education.

This mentorship story is a heartfelt reminder that empowerment isn't always about professional growth or business success—it could be about standing up against social injustice, advocating change and inspiring others to do the same.

These unique stories shed light on how influential mentors can guide their protégés towards remarkable success. The transformative potential of such mentorship relationships extends beyond personal growth and development. They have the power to shape organizations, disrupt industries and even drive societal change. Therefore, fostering empowering mentorships not only develops future leaders but also plays a pivotal role in shaping a more inclusive, innovative and equitable society.

Chapter 12

Integrating Responsibility: How Iconic Leadership Leverages Social Initiatives for Impact

In today's dynamic world, one term increasingly associated with successful leaders is 'iconic'. But what exactly does iconic leadership entail? Iconic leaders are often characterized by their visionary drive, charisma, and an ability to inspire followership. They demonstrate the epitome of excellence and set a benchmark for others in their field. Their actions and decisions characterize them; they create a lasting impact on their organization and people.

However, recently, the definition of iconic leadership has expanded to include a crucial component - Corporate Social Responsibility (CSR). CSR refers to an organization's commitment to assume accountability for its actions on the environment, social wellbeing, and economic prosperity. It manifests from the top—leaders who recognize their organization's role in society and strive to fulfill it are often at the heart of CSR initiatives.

Successful leaders today realize the importance of incorporating CSR within their leadership style. They understand that business profitability should not compromise societal well-being. Hence, many have begun adopting a more 'purpose-driven' leadership approach that seamlessly integrates with Corporate Social Responsibility. This paradigm shift plays a pivotal role in shaping businesses' future to not only be profitable but also socially responsible.

A purpose-driven leader is not just focused on short-term profit margins. Rather, they aim to achieve long-term sustainability by creating value for all stakeholders involved - employees, customers, the community, and shareholders alike. They believe in working towards greater societal good backed by a strong sense of ethics and values. Purpose-driven leaders uphold that businesses can go beyond profits to also serve as agents of positive change. By integrating CSR into their core strategies, these leaders bolster morality, equality, and sustainability in an organization's operations.

Despite the seemingly altruistic nature of such initiatives, it's important to note that CSR is not merely charity work. Its strategic implementation can foster substantial benefits for the company as well. Effective CSR initiatives not only enhance the organization's brand and reputation but also inspire employees, attract top talent, and generate customer loyalty. Therefore, it's no surprise how purpose-driven leadership has evolved into a mainstream business strategy in the 21st century.

The amalgamation of iconic leadership and CSR harnesses a powerful synergy that can significantly influence an organization's success trajectory. Such leaders do more than just running a profitable business; they inspire, motivate, and instill a shared objective for a better world among their workforce. The integration of corporate social responsibility into their iconic leadership narrative therefore serves as the cornerstone of sustainable business practices today.

Next, let's delve deeper into the intertwining of Corporate Social Responsibility (CSR) with iconic leadership. Notably, by integrating CSR in their core ethos, leaders elevate their status to iconic. But how exactly does this integration occur?

There's a unique symbiosis where CSR bolsters the iconic image of leaders. It's achieved when leaders actively participate and advocate for socially responsible initiatives. They align these initiatives with the company's vision and mission, creating a unified objective that permeates every layer of the organization. This alignment sends a decisive message - it's not just about profits but also about making a positive impact on society.

The Harvard Business Review published an insightful case study that revealed how leadership behaviors significantly influence organizational culture. When leaders are seen actively promoting and participating in CSR, it creates a ripple effect throughout the organization, encouraging employees at all levels to commit to such initiatives themselves.

Take Starbucks as an example; under the attackful leadership of Howard Schultz, the company has led various social initiatives over decades. Schultz's belief in 'serving more than just coffee' propelled Starbucks' active participation in causes like employment of veterans, college funding for staff, and ethically sourcing its products. His iconic leadership image is inseparable from this devotion towards societal upliftment.

A leader who consciously integrates CSR into their operational strategy can enhance their iconic image significantly. By championing environmentally friendly processes or advocating for equal opportunity employment, they demonstrate their commitment to social responsibility, which amplifies public perception of them as truly-iconic figures that embody ethical values and principles.

However, it's necessary to note that this association between iconic leadership and CSR transcends mere 'image building'. It isn't another marketing gimmick aimed at enhancing corporate reputation. True integration manifests when leaders adopt forward-thinking perspectives that genuinely consider environmental sustainability and societal wellbeing integral parts of the organization's growth trajectory.

The integration of CSR and iconic leadership dynamically shapes an organization's culture. Employees are inspired to follow leaders who not only aim for profitability but also focus on making a positive societal impact. Their increased investment in the company's vision strengthens their organizational commitment, consequently driving greater productivity and engagement. Ultimately, this influence goes beyond the confines of the organization - it progressively molds public perception about the company as well, helping it earn trust and loyalty from its customer base and shareholders.

In conclusion, integrating Corporate Social Responsibility into their overall strategy is one way that leaders can elevate their status to iconic. It helps cement their position as empathetic figures who go above and beyond mere profitability. By converging societal concerns with business objectives, they foster an ecosystem that balances economic success with social wellbeing, thereby creating a legacy that extends well beyond their tenure.

Now that we have comprehended how iconic leadership and CSR go hand in hand, let's delve into understanding purpose-driven leadership in iconic figures. Purpose-driven leaders are the pioneers of corporate social responsibility, spearheading initiatives that promote societal well-being alongside business growth.

Some of the world's most successful companies owe their achievements to purpose-driven leadership. Google's Larry Page and Sergey Brin, for instance, have been monumental in using their iconic status to bolster the company's commitment to renewable energy. Their focus on sustainable practices is not merely about fulfilling a corporate obligation but deeply ingrained in their vision - making information universally accessible and useful. As an outcome, Google has pledged to be carbon-neutral since 2007.

Similarly, Starbucks' Howard Schultz, another quintessential example of a purpose-driven leader, believes in 'serving more than just coffee'. Schultz embodies his conviction by initiating programs like college funding for employees and ethically sourcing Starbucks products. With this strategy underpinning Starbucks' operations, Schultz ensures the brand reflects a narrative highlighting sustainability and community involvement apart from its regular services.

A study published in the Journal of Corporate Social Responsibility (jcsr) suggests that purpose-driven leaders who emphasize integrating CSR initiatives into strategic plans help facilitate a culture of inclusivity within organizations. Such leaders are characterized by open-mindedness, adaptability, cultural intelligence, and effective collaboration—all essential elements needed to nurture socially responsible initiatives effectively.

Purpose-driven leadership also epitomizes 'inclusive growth,' wherein all stakeholders—employees, partners, consumers, shareholders—are considered pivotal contributors to organizational success. Deloitte Insights outlines inclusive growth as a vital trait of 21st-century leadership that empowers employee development through training programs or inclusive recruitment policies catering to diverse cross-sections of society. Simultaneously, it frames consumer-centric approaches that give back to communities—whether it's through environmental efforts or social initiatives.

Lululemon Athletica is an excellent example where its CEO, Calvin McDonald, has concentrated efforts on promoting physical and mental wellbeing globally. Their initiative to provide free mindfulness and yoga resources to consumers during the COVID-19 pandemic highlights their purpose-driven leadership approach. With this initiative, Lululemon positions itself as a brand that cares about its consumers' holistic health while also driving brand awareness.

The role of a purpose-driven leader extends beyond business profitability. They aim to foster an environment that respects, values, and accounts for all stakeholders' needs. They understand the vitality of integrating CSR effectively into the company's ethos—leading through actions that balance corporate growth with societal wellbeing. By so doing, these leaders enhance their overall brand image and establish their iconic status in the business world.

A key component often overlooked in understanding purpose-driven leadership is persistence—the continuous effort to keep pushing socially responsible agendas even when they're not immediately beneficial. Iconic leaders are visionaries who look beyond short-term gains—they value long-term impacts entailing sustainability and inclusive growth above all else.

In sum, successful organizations often share a common trait —purpose driven figures at their helm championing corporate social responsibility. These leaders believe in founding a legacy marked by sustainable growth and societal well-being—an integral part of their iconic leadership narrative.

Moving forward, let's investigate how socially responsible initiatives influence both an organization and its employees. Commencing with the employees, it is observed that businesses indulging in CSR activities often report higher job satisfaction levels amongst their workers.

Employees feel a sense of pride and satisfaction while working for socially responsible companies. According to a study published online, employees associated with organizations that value ethical responsibilities are more likely to feel proud of their work, loyal to the company, and satisfied with their jobs.

For instance, consider Google's commitment to becoming carbon-neutral since 2007. It's not just about reducing carbon footprints; rather, it's about setting a precedent for other organizations and inspiring change. Employees at Google reportedly have a high level of job satisfaction because they are proud of the socially-conscious work their employer does.

Moreover, by integrating social responsibility into leadership narratives, iconic leaders drive deeper loyalty among the workforce. Such leaders make decisions that benefit the greater society and in the process create an organizational culture where employees feel valued and respected.

Shifting our lens towards the impact on organizations, CSR has been shown to offer several benefits. One such advantage is enhancing business reputation and brand image. Companies that actively invest in CSR programs are often viewed favorably by consumers. For example, let's consider The Coca-Cola Company: through multiple initiatives like water conservation projects and women empowerment programs around the globe, they have improved their public perception considerably.

Socially responsible corporate behavior not only helps cultivate customer loyalty but also contributes to attracting potential investors and partners. Institutional investors are increasingly aware of environmental, social and governance (ESG) criteria when making funding decisions, therefore firms demonstrating commitment in these areas have greater chances of attracting and retaining investment.

Further, CSR programs can also have a positive effect on a company's bottom line. Contrary to common belief that prioritizing societal needs may dilute profitability, data indicates otherwise. Purpose-driven organizations often see increased customer loyalty and improved business performance resulting from their socially responsible initiatives. It reflects in the Sustainability ROI Framework introduced by Bob Willard, a leading expert in corporate sustainability, which lays out how profitability and sustainability are mutually inclusive and not exclusive.

Moreover, it's important to consider the flip side of the coin too: repercussions for businesses ignoring social responsibilities can be severe – from damage to brand image to potential losses associated with consumer boycotts or lawsuits. Companies that fail to act responsibly face backlash from consumers, shareholders and the broader public, which could eventually harm their business prospects.

It is clear that integrating socially responsible initiatives significantly benefits both employees and organizations at large. Employees gain a sense of fulfillment, pride, job satisfaction and loyalty, while for organizations it translates into enhanced brand reputation, customer loyalty, potential for increased profits and reduced risk of public backlash. It reaffirms the imperative for leaders to include Corporate Social Responsibility as an integral part of their strategy; not merely as a box-ticking exercise or peripheral activity but instead actively incorporate it within their core operations.

Now equipped with a profound understanding of the importance of socially responsible initiatives and their impact on both employees and organizations, let's identify some successful examples. These examples will serve as benchmarks for aspiring leaders looking to integrate Corporate Social Responsibility (CSR) into their leadership narrative.

Firstly, take a look at the tech giant, Apple. Under the iconic leadership of Tim Cook, Apple has not only seen remarkable financial growth but also significant strides in its environmental initiatives. Cook has worked diligently to ensure that all Apple facilities run on 100% renewable energy. Not stopping there, he further pledged to make the entire supply chain carbon neutral by 2030, demonstrating an unprecedented commitment to corporate responsibility within the tech industry.

Cook once said, "We don't want to debate climate change. We want to stop it." This vision aligns with Apple's push towards greener products like its latest iPhone models that come without a power adapter—underscoring Cook's aspiration of reducing electronic waste.

Another exemplary company is Nestlé – a brand that resonates globally due to its diverse product portfolio. Nestlé's CEO Mark Schneider made headlines when he declared plastics waste as one of the most pressing issues facing businesses today. The company aims for 100% of its packaging to be recyclable or reusable by 2025 while working towards halving its greenhouse gas emissions over the next decade.

Nestlé also goes beyond in promoting responsible agriculture practices among its suppliers and offers training programs focusing on women entrepreneurs in cocoa-growing regions; showing how CSR forms an integral part of their business operations.

Lululemon Athletica is yet another example showcasing how corporate social responsibility can drastically shape a company's image positively. When faced with the COVID-19 pandemic, Lululemon acted responsibly by closing most physical stores worldwide, but simultaneously provided free online yoga classes and mindfulness resources to the public, supporting their mission to 'enhance people's health and happiness'. Their actions displayed a commitment to the wellbeing of their customers beyond merely selling them products.

Lastly, consider Disney. Known for its enchanting entertainment and a staggering market presence, Disney doesn't shy away from demonstrating its commitment towards CSR either. The enterprise is obsessed with reducing its environmental footprint. They've set ambitious goals like sending zero waste to landfills by 2020 and reducing net emissions by 50% from 2012 levels. Furthermore, they've launched initiatives aimed at conservation education worldwide through the Disney Conservation Fund—in this way, effectively intertwining their corporate responsibility agenda with their iconic leadership narrative.

In each of these cases we observe that Corporate Social Responsibility isn't an afterthought—it is meticulously woven into the company's business strategy. Adopting such an approach doesn't just contribute towards societal progress but also drives distinct advantages for these firms, including boosted brand reputation, enhanced employee satisfaction and increased loyalty among consumers.

Chapter 13

Adaptability and Evolution: Icons in a Changing Landscape

In today's fast-paced, ever-evolving world, it is clear that adaptability is not merely a beneficial trait, but an essential one. This holds true across every sphere of life, but nowhere more so than in leadership. Iconic leadership, to be precise. To understand why this is so, one must first comprehend the intricate relationship between adaptability and iconic leadership.

What makes a leader iconic? Is it their vision, charisma, ability to inspire? While all these qualities are undoubtedly crucial, another equally significant yet often underplayed factor comes into play - adaptability. Statistics and real-world examples confirm this repeatedly. Those leaders who have been able to sustain their impact over time and remain relevant amidst changing landscapes have demonstrated exceptional adaptability skills. They have proven that they are capable of not just enduring change, but harnessing it for growth.

Understanding this brings us to a pivotal question: Why is the importance of adaptability so pronounced in the context of iconic leadership? The answer can be found in the very nature of our ever-changing landscape.

Whether we look at politics, economics or technology, change is the only constant. If we specifically talk about the business world where most leadership roles exist, change cements itself as an even more integral part of the landscape. Market forces fluctuate, customer preferences transform, laws and regulations evolve, technology advances by leaps and bounds, creating a milieu of permutations and combinations that hit businesses hard and fast. It's in such a changing landscape where adaptability comes into play.

A leader without the ability to adapt would soon find themselves and their organization outpaced by those more attuned to these shifts. An iconic leader though is always thinking ahead, preparing their team for what's on the horizon, and equipping them to thrive, not merely survive. This ability to anticipate and adapt to changes is what keeps them staying ahead of the curve, keeping their leadership image intact and iconic.

This brings us to another critical aspect of this discussion – staying ahead of the curve doesn't happen by chance. It takes a keen eye for recognizing patterns, an open mind willing to learn and unlearn, and a dogged determination to lead with conviction even in uncertain times.

Maintaining an iconic leadership image isn't a one-time achievement; it demands constant evolution and adaptation. Embracing change and staying ahead of the curve, therefore, becomes imperative for anyone aspiring towards iconic leadership.

Dive into changing dynamics

In the throes of our rapidly evolving world, the only certainty is uncertainty. This incertitude intensifies in the business domain where trends, preferences, and operations are subject to incessant modification. Crucial among these continual revisions is technology. Technological advancements have a sweeping and profound impact on every aspect of how businesses operate and serve their customers.

Think about it: companies now can interact with their customers directly through various digital platforms, collect real-time data about market trends, utilize Artificial Intelligence for decision making, and much more. Technologies like blockchain, Internet of Things (IoTs), virtual reality, machine learning are reshaping industries every day. Therefore an iconic leader should not just understand these changes but stay ahead by leveraging them proactively within their organization.

This brings us to a secondary yet equally important aspect of leadership adaptability - continuous learning. The rate at which technology is advancing necessitates leaders to stay up-to-date with emerging trends continually. Garnering new knowledge becomes crucial as old ways lose relevance quickly, replaced by newer, agile methodologies. However, continuous learning isn't solely about acquiring new technical know-how; it also involves fostering an open mindset that invites fresh perspectives and encourages innovation.

An iconic leader promotes this culture of constant acquisition and application of knowledge throughout their team or organization. Such an environment encourages everyone to upgrade themselves continuously – to never stop learning. In other words, iconic leadership doesn't merely adapt to change individually; they inspire a collective effort to embrace change and learn from it organically.

This discipline creates a workforce that stays informed about industry transformations and anticipates them instead of merely reacting to them after they occur. And when people in an organization learn together – they grow together too. This shared journey fortifies teamwork and boosts efficiency.

A key factor that fuels this dynamic of continuous learning is curiosity. The willingness to ask questions, challenge existing notions, and explore novel pathways is an essential prerequisite to learning consistently. An iconic leader nurtures this trait within their team creating an environment where questioning and exploring are not merely accepted, but encouraged.

To sum up, navigating through continually changing dynamics necessitates two intertwined components: comprehension of technological advancements and the fostering of continuous organizational and personal learning. Both work in unison - leaders who stay updated with technical evolutions can guide their teams better, and teams armed with a culture of learning can leverage technological changes more proficiently.

The end result? An adaptable leadership that maneuvers through volatile industry changes effectively whilst maintaining an iconic leadership image – a beacon of stability amidst chaos guided by insight, innovation, and foresight.

Crucial Actions to Successful Adaptation

The ability to navigate through industry changes effectively is an integral part of iconic leadership. However, doing so requires more than just recognition of the change at hand. It demands a calculated strategy, driven by grace and foresight. Leaders who exhibit grace under pressure are often those that can inspire their teams amidst turbulent times.

In truth, adapting to new industry trends doesn't have to be a struggle; it can be a strategic maneuver. By staying well-informed about industry developments, iconic leaders position themselves to make decisions proactively versus responsively. They anticipate changes, prepare for them and guide their teams through them seamlessly.

Foresight in leadership goes hand-in-hand with adaptability. Forward-thinking leaders keep an eye on future trends and strategize accordingly, ensuring they're not only ready when the changes arrive but already steps ahead of the curve. This kind of proactive approach creates a buffer against sudden industry upheavals and allows organizations to navigate change efficiently.

Iconic leaders also empower their teams during periods of change by fostering open communication and transparency. Keeping everyone in the loop about what's happening, why it's happening, how it affects them, and what's being done about it creates an environment of trust. This trust makes a major difference when navigating industry changes.

At times, these changes may require learning new skills or adopting new methodologies - both of which can be met with resistance if not handled delicately. Iconic leaders anticipate this resistance and lead with empathy, understanding that people need time to adjust to new ways of doing things. These leaders provide necessary training resources, offer patience as team members learn and grow, and encourage rather than criticize during the transitional phase.

Moreover, iconic leadership isn't shy about leaning on external benchmark references. There's no harm in learning from others. Observing how other businesses are navigating industry changes, especially your direct competitors, can give you fresh insights and ideas on how to tackle the same challenges within your organization. While every company's context may be unique, some strategies are universally effective.

Ultimately, leading with grace and foresight during times of change is about maintaining balance. It's about striking the right chord between becoming future-ready and managing daily operations. It means being receptive to new market shifts while still delivering consistent value to customers. This multi-faceted approach ensures that no matter how volatile or unpredictable the landscape becomes, an iconic leader will always find their footing and guide their team forward.

In conclusion, successfully navigating through industry changes requires a few crucial actions: staying well-informed about trends, communicating transparently with teams, demonstrating patience and support during transitional phases, learning from others, and maintaining daily operations without compromising the vision for the future. These practices embody the essence of adaptability and form the cornerstone of iconic leadership.

The Benefits of Successful Adaptation

Successful adaptation in leadership offers a plethora of benefits that extend far beyond merely surviving change. It paves the way for growth, resilience and continued success. Most importantly, it contributes to fostering an iconic leadership image that doesn't merely weather the storm of change, but uses it as a catalyst for innovation and progress.

One of the most profound benefits is enhanced position and credibility within your field or industry. Leaders who demonstrate adaptability in their decision-making process and strategic direction are often seen as visionaries, able to anticipate shifts in the market before they occur. They are highly respected and admired not only by their team but by their competitors, customers, partners and stakeholders too.

Another significant benefit lies in strengthening organizational agility. When leaders fully embrace adaptability, it permeates every level of their organization. They create agile teams who can quickly pivot strategies or processes as needed based on real-time feedback or sudden market shifts. This agility enhances performance in today's unpredictable business climate where abilities to react swiftly can be a major competitive advantage.

This agility also promotes innovation. When you're willing to adapt, you're open to new ideas, methodologies and ways of thinking - both from within your organization and externally. Often this openness prompts creative solutions to challenges, which can result in improved products/services or more efficient ways of working.

Adaptive leaders also excel in decision making during uncertain times. They understand that calculated risks often pave the way for substantial rewards. Rather than being paralyzed by fear when faced with difficult decisions, such leaders confidently take action using available data and intuition. They accept failures if encountered as learning opportunities rather than catastrophes.

Beyond internal benefits, successfully adapting contributes to building trust with your external network – clients/customers and partners alike. Those who show up consistently, adapting to serve their customers best even in challenging times, build a reputation for reliability and commitment. They secure customer loyalty – a key component in driving business success.

There's also an undeniable effect on problem-solving abilities. When the status quo is regularly challenged by changes, leaders get plenty of opportunities to hone their problem-solving prowess. The need to strategize and execute plans amidst constant change sharpens one's skills for critical analysis, innovation and resilience - all integral components of effective problem-solving.

Moreover, the learning curve that comes from successful adaptation is invaluable. Every situation navigated successfully leaves behind lessons learned both from victories and mistakes made along the way. This accumulated wisdom better prepares you for future challenges.

In conclusion, while staying adaptable in leadership may pose its own challenges, its benefits far outweigh them. From enhanced positions within industry ranks, greater organizational agility to improved problem-solving abilities - these are but some perks that come with successful adaptation. But perhaps the most valuable win is earning the coveted title of 'iconic leader', revered not just for their adaptability but for leading with vision, grace and foresight amidst continual change.

Case Studies throughout Time

Historical case studies offer a wealth of insights into the concept of adaptability and iconic leadership. Leaders from different sectors have time and again showcased that these two elements are not merely correlated but deeply intertwined, shaping leaders' legacies and influencing their companies' trajectories. Let's delve into some remarkable examples showcasing the effectiveness of adapting to change.

Apple Inc: The Visionary Shifts of Steve Jobs

No conversation about adaptability is complete without the mention of Apple Inc's late co-founder, Steve Jobs. Over his tenure as CEO, he transformed Apple into one of the most valuable brands globally by adapting swiftly to changing consumer needs and technological advancements.

In 2001, when digital music was just emerging, Jobs anticipated its impact on how people consume music. Recognizing an opportunity, he led Apple in creating the iPod - a product departure from their regular computer offerings but one that would redefine portable music and pave the path for future innovations like the iPhone and iPad. This ability to foresee industry changes and move dynamically is a testament to Job's iconic leadership.

Satya Nadella: Revitalizing Microsoft

Another tech giant who exemplifies adaptability in leadership is Satya Nadella, current CEO of Microsoft. When he assumed his role in 2014, Microsoft was struggling with declining PC sales while failing to gain significant traction in mobile space.

Nadella quickly pivoted Microsoft's strategy toward 'cloud-first, mobile-first', recognizing cloud computing's future importance. He adapted both his personal leadership style and corporate strategy to embrace open-source technology despite past company norms. As a result, Microsoft has regained its position among tech titans mainly due to its successful cloud services business.

Mary Barra: Driving Change at General Motors

Mary Barra, CEO of General Motors (GM), is another iconic leader who has adeptly steered her company through significant industry changes. Facing a shifting landscape towards electric vehicles and self-driving technology, Barra pivoted GM's strategy to focus on these new areas.

Under her leadership, GM has committed to 30 all-electric models by the end of 2025 and aims for carbon neutrality by 2040. These bold moves in adapting to industry shifts have positioned GM on the frontlines of the automotive industry's future.

Inclusive leadership is another area where Barra has shown adaptability as she strives to create an inclusive culture within the traditionally male-dominated auto industry. She stands as an example of a leader who recognizes societal changes and adapts accordingly to move her organization forward.

Sir Richard Branson: Embracing Risk and Innovation

Sir Richard Branson, founder of the Virgin Group, embodies adaptability with his diverse portfolio spanning from music records to airlines to space travel. Branson has built his career on taking calculated risks in new industries - embodying the spirit of adapting to change while innovating relentlessly.

Despite numerous failures along the way, Branson's willingness to adapt his strategies based on lessons learned has been instrumental in his overall success as an entrepreneur. He symbolizes how adaptability coupled with resilience can deliver impressive results over time.

These inspiring leaders from varied backgrounds illustrate that adaptability is crucial irrespective of industry or time period. It's clear that iconic leadership thrives on adapting to change, using it as a vehicle for innovation, growth, and sustainable success.

Chapter 14

Iconic Team Dynamics: Strategies for Fostering Collaboration and Innovation

Although some of these areas may have been touched upon let's look at them again in the context of iconic team membership, specifically how to foster collaboration and innovation with dynamic teams.

Team dynamics are the unseen forces that operate in a team between different groups of people. They can significantly impact how a team reacts, behaves, and performs, and they can pose both substantial challenges as well as provide unique opportunities for enhancing team performance. The idea of 'Iconic Team Dynamics' refers to the positive force created by a well-tuned team, directed towards fostering collaboration and innovation, which paves the path for success in any organizational setting.

The uniqueness of iconic team dynamics lies in its ability to transcend beyond the traditional concept of teamwork. It encapsulates the elements of fostering collaboration, *'building a cohesive team'*, creating an innovative environment, and generating an *'idea-sharing environment'*. It is all about applying strategic measures to facilitate effective interaction amongst team members, thereby aligning individual goals and objectives with the organization's vision and mission.

Fostering collaboration involves integrating diverse perspectives, knowledge, and skills from individuals within the team to achieve common goals. Collaboration fosters creativity, learning, and innovation, making it an essential tool for solving complex problems and generating new ideas.

Another fundamental aspect revolves around *'building a cohesive team'*. This references a series of processes designed to integrate employees into the organisational culture and value system. This kind of integration is achieved by promoting shared decision-making, open communication, trust-building, respect for diversity and shared commitment towards achieving organisational goals. Building a cohesive team enhances team spirit, productivity, and overall efficiency.

The notion of an *'Innovative team'* pertains to teams that regularly produce novel ideas and solutions. These teams foster a culture of risk-taking, where ideas are freely exchanged without fear of criticism or ridicule. Innovative teams are not just about inventing new things; they also excel at identifying and implementing improvements to existing processes or systems.

Considering these elements, Iconic Team Dynamics becomes a strategic approach to enhancing team productivity and effectiveness. It transcends the usual parameters of simple teamwork by fostering a proactive environment conducive to collaboration, innovation, and success.\nThe transformative journey from traditional teamwork to iconic team dynamics is not a straightforward endeavor. It demands clarity in vision, effective leadership, commitment from all team members, the right strategies, and techniques, along with an enabling environment that fosters creativity and innovation.

The Role of an Iconic Leader

Central to the narrative of iconic team dynamics is the presence of an 'iconic leader'. They perform a pivotal role in shaping, curating, and orchestrating these dynamic teams. An iconic leader goes beyond the conventional understanding of leadership; they embody certain characteristics that set them apart from others. They command respect, inspire, and motivate teams through their visions, actions, and ethical principles making them a key catalyst in fostering collaboration and innovation.

An iconic leader often exhibits high emotional intelligence which enables them to comprehend, sympathize with, and motivate individuals within their team. This fosters a strong bond, mutual respect and amplifies trust within the group leading to a more *'cohesive team'*. They are frequently skilled communicators who can articulate their vision succinctly ensuring everyone in the team understands their individual roles in fulfilling this vision.

Iconic leaders also play a vital part in building an 'innovative team'. They cultivate an environment where ideas feel valued and are freely shared amongst teammates. Their willingness to take risks creates an atmosphere for people to think outside the box without fearing failure or retribution because they understand that risk-taking is intrinsic to innovation. More importantly, they show appreciation for creative thinking by recognizing and rewarding novel ideas.

Sometimes it can be beneficial to reflect on real-life examples of such iconic leaders who have helped shape successful teams. Steve Jobs is one such emblematic figure whose leadership transformed Apple Inc into an icon of innovation. He nurtured a culture that encouraged innovation by fostering collaboration and open communication within teams while constantly challenging them to 'think different'. Jobs' ability to drive his teams towards realizing his vision led to groundbreaking products like Macintosh, iPhone and iPad among many others.

Another strong example of an iconic leader is Elon Musk. Known for his audacious goals and radical approach, he has continuously pushed his teams at SpaceX and Tesla to defy traditional norms and boundaries. Thanks to his leadership style, these organizations are renowned for their innovative solutions despite facing steep challenges. Musk's leadership fosters a culture that encourages risk-taking and embraces failure as a stepping-stone towards success. His ability to inspire his workforce in the pursuit of seemingly impossible goals stands testament to the power an iconic leader holds in shaping team dynamics.

However, it is necessary to acknowledge that while iconic leaders play a fundamental role in forming and guiding dynamic teams, true collaboration and innovation require commitment from all members of the team. Every individual within the team needs to align with the common vision set by the leader, be open to sharing ideas without fearing judgement, appreciate diversity of thought, and be willing to work collaboratively.

Therefore, effective leadership from an iconic figure coupled with commitment from team members aids in fostering collaboration and innovation leading to 'Iconic Team Dynamics'.

Strategies & Methods for fostering Iconic Team Dynamics

To establish a work environment which stimulates iconic team dynamics, both leaders and organizations need to implement certain strategies and practices. These methods should encourage collaboration, foster innovation, and lay the foundation for strong, cohesive teams.

'Creating an environment for collaboration' requires strategic planning and implementation. A key aspect is building a supportive infrastructure that enables easy communication and ideation amongst the team members. This could be achieved by creating physical spaces meant for collaborative work or incorporating digital tools like project management apps to facilitate seamless interaction, especially in remote working conditions.

Moreover, collaboration can also be enhanced through activities such as regular team meetings where everyone has an equal opportunity to put forward their ideas, brainstorming sessions aimed at solving specific problems or generating new ideas, and workshops or training programs designed to build teamwork skills. Organizations may also consider implementing team-building activities such as problem-solving quests or leadership exercises to help strengthen relationships within the team.

Similarly, 'fostering innovation' requires cultivating an organizational culture that values risk-taking and creativity. Leaders need to instill an atmosphere where ideas are encouraged rather than dismissed out of hand due to perceived risks or conflicts with established norms. One way to foster innovative thinking is through structured brainstorming sessions where employees are given freedom to explore all ideas without judgement. Organizations should also provide room for experimentation wherein employees can validate their concepts through pilot projects or prototypes.

Apart from fostering a conducive environment, another strategy involves harnessing diverse skill-sets within the team. Teams composed of individuals with diverse backgrounds bring different perspectives to the table which can enrich idea generation process and innovation. Hence, leaders should strive to build diversity in their teams not just in terms of professional background but also gender, age, cultural backgrounds etc.

Additionally, it is essential to build a system for recognizing and rewarding innovation. This not only motivates employees but also instills a sense of ownership encouraging them to contribute more effectively towards team goals. Rewards need not be financial always, even recognition in front of peers or assigning lead roles in projects can act as great motivators.

In conclusion, fostering iconic team dynamics requires a strategic approach that combines creating an environment conducive for collaboration, encouraging innovation, leveraging diversity and recognizing efforts. In doing so, leaders and organizations can unlock the potential of their teams and drive sustained growth and success.

Case Studies: Insights into Successful Iconic Team Dynamics

While understanding the theoretical approach to iconic team dynamics is critical, it is equally important to look at practical applications. We shall now delve into a few case studies that demonstrate the successful implementation of these principles.

Case Study 1: Google's Project Aristotle

The first study references tech giant Google's 'Project Aristotle'. The company undertook an extensive research project to understand the dynamics behind their most successful teams and found that it wasn't just about gathering the best individual talents. Instead, they discovered that psychological safety - an environment where all team members feel safe to take risks and be vulnerable in front of each other - was foundational for fostering collaboration and innovation.

Case Study 2: Airbnb's Cultural Transformation

Airbnb provides another excellent example when it comes to creating a culture of innovation amidst crisis. When faced with bankruptcy in its early days, instead of cutting corners, CEO Brian Chesky implemented steps to foster creativity within his team. This led Airbnb to pivot from merely a booking site to delivering unique experiences -- turning its fortunes around.

Case Study 3: Spotify's Agile Model

Spotify has been consistently praised for its innovative organizational structure known as Spotify's model of Agile squads, which promotes autonomy in decision-making while also ensuring alignment toward common goals. Each squad operates independently but collectively support Spotify's overall strategy. This way, they maintain a balance between individual innovation and corporate cohesion, a hallmark of iconic team dynamics.

Case Study 4: Pixar's Creative Collaboration

Pixar Animation Studios is renowned for its culture of creativity and collaboration. Co-founder Ed Catmull established the 'Pixar Braintrust,' a group of creative leaders who critique ongoing projects in a constructive manner. By creating an environment that supports candid discussions and valuing different perspectives, Pixar has been able to produce some of the most innovative movies in the animation industry.(source)

In each of these case studies, it's clear that effective leadership, strategic efforts towards fostering collaboration and creating an environment conducive to innovation have led to successful outcomes. The principles of iconic team dynamics have manifested in various forms, customised according to each organisation's unique characteristics.

However, it's important to remember that all successful teams are works-in-progress. They continuously learn, adapt and evolve their strategies to stay innovative in the face of change. As such, iconic team dynamics isn't just about implementing certain strategies; it's about nurturing a mindset that values collaboration and celebrates innovation.

Promoting Collaboration and Innovation Amidst Conflict

While the concept of iconic team dynamics advocates for collaboration and innovation, it is essential to recognize that teams are not devoid of conflicts. Different individuals bring diverse ideas and perspectives on the table; disagreements are bound to occur. However, managed appropriately, these conflicts can indeed serve as potential catalysts for fostering creativity and innovation.

As counterintuitive as it may sound, conflict in teams is not necessarily a negative thing. In fact, a certain degree of conflict can stimulate critical thinking and challenge status quo, eventually leading to innovative solutions. The key lies not in the absence of conflict but in how such disagreements are managed and redirected towards productive outcomes. This requires an environment where different opinions are encouraged and respected instead of being suppressed.

'Iconic leaders' play a vital role here - their approach towards handling team conflicts sets the tone for its resolution. Instead of imposing their ideas or decisions, an iconic leader would facilitate discussions around conflicting ideas, encouraging all members to express their views openly. By doing this, they foster an 'idea-sharing environment' where everyone feels heard and valued.

In situations where disagreements persist even after thorough discussions, leaders should focus on finding common ground rather than insisting on a unanimous decision. Sometimes, it is also beneficial to get external help in resolving conflicts such as through mediators or professional conflict resolution experts.

Beyond just resolving conflicts, another important aspect is learning from them. Leaders should encourage reflection post-conflict resolution process to understand what led to the conflict and how it was resolved. These learnings provide valuable insights which can be used for better management of future conflicts.

The Value of Psychological Safety

A cornerstone in managing team conflicts effectively lies in establishing psychological safety within the team. Psychological safety refers to a shared belief that the team is safe for interpersonal risk-taking. In other words, team members feel confident that they won't be punished or ridiculed for speaking up, asking questions, freely expressing their thoughts, or admitting mistakes.

Teams with high psychological safety are more likely to stay resilient in the face of conflict and bounce back stronger. This concept goes hand in hand with fostering collaboration and innovation as it allows individuals to share their ideas freely, take risks in implementing novel solutions and learn from their failures without fear of judgement.

The role of leaders is critical in cultivating psychological safety within teams, which involves displaying traits of empathy, trustworthiness, transparency and openness. They need to lead by example – showing vulnerability, openly acknowledging their mistakes and appreciating others who do the same. Leaders should also actively encourage participation from all members during meetings and discussions which would instill confidence among the team that their contributions matter.

Turning Conflict into Collaboration

To summarize, conflicts will inevitably arise within dynamic teams due to diversity in perspectives and ideas. However, managed effectively through a culture of psychological safety and open communication, these conflicts can be turned into breeding grounds for creativity and innovation. By navigating through conflicts constructively, iconic leaders foster an environment where differences are leveraged towards driving progress rather than causing discordance - thereby promoting a healthy growth-oriented narrative around disputes within 'iconic team dynamics'.

Chapter 15

Iconicity beyond the Office: A Personal Touch

In our highly connected world, leadership has evolved beyond exerting influence within the confines of traditional office spaces. Iconic leadership persona have extended their impact not merely in professional settings but also in personal interactions and social spheres. These are the leaders who transcend the boundaries of their roles to make a difference on a broader scale, leaving lasting impressions wherever they go.

'Iconic Leadership', as the term proposes, speaks to the individuals who command respect and admiration in their respective fields due to their unparalleled vision, charisma, and, importantly, their authenticity. They are the ones who inspire others through their actions, way of handling situations, and most prominently by remaining true to their character. Their influence is not limited to the business or organizational contexts; they leave indelible imprints on their followers' minds through casual personal interactions as well.

However, being this iconic figure does not come effortlessly. It's a constant journey that requires commitment to one's identity while balancing it with professional obligations - a task easier said than done. Yet, the leaders who accomplish this balance set an example for others to follow.

So why does this type of leadership matter? What makes it stand out amongst various kinds of leadership styles?

The answer lies in its profound impact - not just on a team or an organization but extending towards wider societal structures. Such leaders often create an ecosystem around them that fosters creativity, innovation while maintaining an environment of mutual respect. And these virtues do not restrict themselves within office premises; they flow into the personal lives of those influenced by such leaders.

Beyond the positive organizational growth, this sort of leadership encourages personal growth as well. Those working under iconic leaders often find themselves adopting certain qualities and traits that help them in their personal strides as well.

An example worth mentioning here is the late Steve Jobs, co-founder of Apple. His passion for innovation and a keen eye for detail almost single-handedly shaped the course of the tech industry. Even years after his demise, his iconic leadership persona remains an inspiration for many emerging leaders across various industries. However, remember that his charisma was not confined to his professional endeavors; his personal interactions were equally impactful.

Iconic leadership, therefore, is not just about creating successful organizations; it's about leaving an enduring legacy that continues to shape minds and actions, even in personal spheres. It reflects a holistic approach to leadership, focusing on influencing individuals beyond professional boundaries and facilitating overall growth. As we delve deeper into this concept in subsequent sections, we will further explore how iconic leaders balance their professional identity with authenticity in social and community settings and the holistic impact they have.

Leadership does not confine itself within the four walls of an office; it flows seamlessly into our personal lives, shaping how we navigate various situations. The leaders who manage to extend their leadership personas beyond workspaces are the ones who leave a lasting impact on their followers. They are the iconic figures whose influence transcends professional boundaries and enters into the realm of personal interactions.

A classic example of such a leader emerges from the annals of history, none other than Mahatma Gandhi. Known as the 'Father of the Nation' in India, Gandhi used non-violence and peace as his tools to lead India towards independence from British rule. He may not have held any official position or title, but his charismatic leadership made him an icon revered by billions worldwide even today.

Gandhi's persona was not restricted to political movements or freedom struggles. Even in his day-to-day personal interactions, he exhibited humility and adherence to truth which were also his core principles in public life. His modest attire, simple living habits and empathic conversations reflected authenticity that was deeply admired and respected by people across all walks of life. Gandhi's life was a true testament to the power of iconic leadership that does not halt at professional endeavours but continues impressively into personal spaces.

In contemporary times too, we have many examples where leaders extend well beyond their professional roles and make meaningful contributions to their communities and society at large. Take Bill Gates for instance. Known for co-founding Microsoft, Gates is equally recognized for his philanthropic endeavors outside of his professional life. With initiatives like The Bill & Melinda Gates Foundation, he has leveraged his success and resources towards addressing global issues related to health and education.

In both cases - Gandhi and Gates - we see how their actions outside their professional roles shaped their leadership personas significantly. Their personal interactions and actions not only mirrored their core values but also enhanced their credibility and respect among followers. Such is the power of iconic leadership that extends far beyond the corridors of an office.

But what's important to note here is, these leaders did not just act out of impulse or temporary bouts of goodwill. Their personal interactions were a reflection of their overall persona, revealing a consistency that was ingrained in their character. This consistency, be it Gandhi's resolve for non-violence or Gate's commitment towards philanthropy, emerged as a critical part of their leadership personas.

Their individual narratives are proof of how influential iconic leaders can be when they extend their reach beyond workspaces. By consistently living up to their principles in personal settings, they reinforce the trust and belief people have in them. Thus, reiterating the impressionable role of iconic leaders within personal spaces is essentially acknowledging the profound influence they have on shaping societal norms and behavior above and beyond professional contexts.

As we delve deeper into the discourse of iconic leadership, a key aspect that begs further exploration is how these leaders balance their professional identity with their personal authenticity. In other words, how do they manage this high-wire act of being true to their selves while also fulfilling professional obligations and expectations?

Iconic leaders understand that the essence of leadership is not just about achieving organizational goals but also about being genuine and relatable. The latter can only be achieved when leaders maintain their authenticity in every sphere of their lives - professional and personal.

Consider here the case of Sheryl Sandberg, Chief Operating Officer at Facebook. Aside from her role as a top executive in one of the world's largest social media platforms, she is also known for her advocacy towards gender equality, both within and outside the workplace. She famously uses her own experiences to highlight issues faced by women at work through her book 'Lean In' and associated foundation. Sandberg's fight for gender equality may not directly relate to her daily job functions at Facebook, but it certainly forms a significant part of her identity.

In this context, it becomes evident how Sandberg manages to balance her professional persona with her personal cause. Her dedication to promote female empowerment does not interfere with her responsibilities at Facebook; instead, it augments her image as an influential leader who cares about social issues. This authentic stand on a cause enhances respect towards her and shapes people's perception about her leadership style in a positive way.

Maintaining this fine balance between professional and personal identities demands immense integrity and conscious effort from a leader. A deviation from authenticity could easily lead to a credibility crisis amongst followers or peers. Hence, it's important to remember that this balance should not veer towards pretense or insincerity.

Imagine, for instance, if Sheryl Sandberg advocated for gender equality in public but failed to promote similar values within Facebook, then her authenticity and consequently, her leadership effectiveness would be under scrutiny.

Much like a high-wire act, balancing professional identity and personal authenticity is a constant endeavor that requires attention to detail, sensitivity towards followers' perception, and most importantly, unwavering adherence to one's core principles. While this balance might seem like a daunting task, it often serves as the cornerstone of effective iconic leadership.

In truth, becoming an iconic leader goes beyond delivering success stories at their organizations; it also involves leading an authentic life that resonates with others and inspires them to do the same. It's about being genuine in one's actions, consistent in one's approach, and committed to shaping a better world through personal example.

In the arena of iconic leadership, authenticity doesn't merely play a role - it's the cornerstone. This attribute is not confined within office spaces but extends its influence into social and community settings. Here, an iconic leader stakes their reputation not just on professional achievements, but also on their authentic conduct and contribution in these settings.

Authenticity in this context refers to the embodiment of one's core values, principles, beliefs, and ethics consistently across various spheres of life. It is about being genuine, transparent, and relatable; these are traits that create trust and respect amongst followers and peers alike.

A shining example of this virtue is Oprah Winfrey, the iconic American media executive and philanthropist. Despite her towering success in television, she never allowed fame to distort her personal identity. She has been candid about her struggles from childhood through adulthood, opening up avenues for empathetic conversations on various societal issues such as racial discrimination, poverty, and gender inequality.

This authenticity transcends into her philanthropic endeavors too. Oprah's Angel Network has raised more than $80 million for charitable programs including girls' education in South Africa and relief to victims of natural disasters. Her actions parallel her words, leading to a heightened level of trust among millions of people globally who admire her relentless commitment towards making a difference.

Oprah's persona underlines one critical component - when leaders are genuine in their interactions beyond professional boundaries; they enjoy a higher degree of credibility while fostering a stronger emotional connection with their audience or followers. They become role models who inspire people by not just what they achieve professionally but also how they navigate their personal lives authentically.

On the contrary, leaders who fail to demonstrate sincerity outside their professional roles can find it hard to earn respect or trust from others. A leader known for promoting fitness in the workplace but leading an unhealthy lifestyle outside work, for instance, can quickly lose credibility. Authenticity, thus, becomes a critical measure of an iconic leader's impact in social and community settings.

However, it is vital to mention that authenticity shouldn't be mistaken as revealing all aspects of one's personal life publicly. It is about being clear on one's core values and ensuring that actions across different spheres reflect these values consistently.

Leaders like Oprah have shown us that integrity and honesty are at the heart of authentic leadership. As we navigate various roles in our lives - as professionals, friends, spouses, parents, community members – embodying these virtues consistently helps us to maintain our authenticity.

Ultimately, an iconic leader understands their role goes beyond professional obligations. They strive to create a positive impact not just within their organizations but also in society at large. Their attitude towards social issues, their conduct in community scenarios, and even casual personal interactions are often laced with the same level of sincerity and commitment they deliver at work. For them, living authentically is not a choice - it's the way of life.

As we delve further into the understanding of iconic leadership, we must consider the full scope and reach of such leaders. It is not merely in their immediate professional environment that their influence is felt but extends well beyond. The inspirational spark they ignite is not dimmed by the walls of their offices, it continues to burn bright in both professional and personal spheres. We will now explore this holistic impact of an iconic leader.

An iconic leader can be compared to a stone tossed in a pond - as each ripple spreads outwards, it reaches further and impacts even the farthest corners. But these effects aren't haphazard or random – they are precise, measured, and carry the same force as their source.

Elon Musk, CEO of Tesla Inc. and SpaceX, certainly exhibits this holistic influence. In his professional capacity, he has transformed the automotive industry with Tesla's innovative electric cars and disrupted space travel with SpaceX's reusable rockets. This drive for innovation stretches into his personal pursuits too - whether discussing ambitious plans about colonizing Mars or engaging in thought-provoking dialogues on AI governance, Musk stimulates change on multiple fronts.

This example illustrates how an iconic leader like Musk cannot only steer companies towards success but also inspire individuals across various disciplines. His appetite for risk-taking and unperturbed focus resonates with many aspiring entrepreneurs and enthusiasts who aspire to create significant impact amidst challenges.

However, one shouldn't mistake the holistic impact of an iconic leader merely as an extension of their professional bravura into personal life. It's more evolved than that. It reflects their ability to touch different aspects of life through their virtues, actions, decisions while maintaining a consistent image that aligns with their core values.

The case of the late Dame Anita Roddick, founder of The Body Shop International Limited stands as a powerful testament to this. Her unique approach to creating natural and ethically sourced beauty products revolutionized the cosmetics industry. On a personal level, she was an ardent environmental activist known for her firm stance against animal testing and promotion of fair-trade practices.

The holistic impact here was seen in her able to infuse these socially conscious values not only into The Body Shop's operations but also into the minds of consumers who began to care about ethical sourcing, animal rights and environmental conservation because they were buying from a brand that stood for these causes. It isn't just the business world where Roddick left her mark - it extended into society as well by encouraging mindful consumption habits.

Therefore, evaluating an iconic leader's influence beyond professional success requires us to consider their overall contribution – whether it's sparking dialogue on unexplored subjects or promoting critical societal changes. The effectiveness of such leaders is encapsulated in their ability to seamlessly integrate their professional commitments with their personal beliefs and spread similar principles across the various spheres they touch.

An iconic leader then is not just someone who can manage a successful company; he or she can inspire change at multiple levels through consistency between their actions and core values, facilitating positive transformations irrespective of the sphere they are operating within.

Chapter 16

Measuring Iconic Impact: Metrics beyond the Bottom Line

In the ever-evolving corporate landscape, organizations have recognized the importance of prioritizing employee engagement to foster a thriving and motivated workforce. Employee engagement tools have emerged as crucial resources for measuring employees' sentiments towards their workplace culture, creating emotional connections, and driving their commitment to their teams and organizations. Engaged employees not only contribute to the company's overall growth but also demonstrate higher productivity and profitability. In fact, highly engaged teams have been shown to exhibit 21% greater profitability than others, according to Forbes.

This comprehensive guide will delve deeper into the significance of measuring employee engagement metrics and provide insights into key metrics to consider in order to gauge and enhance employee engagement. We will explore the three key aspects of measuring employee engagement, discuss the best KPIs for measuring engagement, and provide practical strategies for measuring employee engagement. Additionally, we will examine the various benefits of tracking employee engagement metrics and provide guidance on what to do after measuring these metrics.

What are Employee Engagement Metrics?

Employee engagement metrics serve as indicators that HR and people leaders utilize to measure and track the level of engagement within their workforce. These metrics encompass a range of factors, including employees' emotional connection to the organization, personal wellness, job satisfaction, workplace relationships, and employee recognition. By quantifying these metrics, organizations can gain valuable insights to develop effective employee engagement strategies and take tangible actions to sustain or improve overall workplace engagement.

To accurately measure employee engagement metrics, organizations often rely on employee engagement surveys. These surveys provide an efficient means of collecting feedback from employees, allowing them to express their feelings about their team, manager, and the organization as a whole. By ensuring anonymity, these surveys encourage employees to provide transparent and honest feedback, which is essential for understanding the current state of engagement within the organization and implementing necessary interventions.

Key Employee Engagement Metrics to Consider

To effectively measure employee engagement, it is crucial to track key metrics that provide a comprehensive view of the workforce's engagement levels. Here are 13 key employee engagement metrics that organizations should consider:

1. Employee Net Promoter Score (eNPS): This classic metric gauges employee satisfaction by asking, "How likely are you to recommend our company as a place to work?" It categorizes employees as Promoters, Passives, or Detractors, providing a clear picture of overall engagement.

2. Employee Satisfaction (ESAT): ESAT surveys gather insights into employee happiness, helping identify areas that need improvement. Happy employees are more likely to be engaged.

3. Employee Turnover Rate: High turnover can signal problems with engagement. Monitoring this metric is crucial as it is costly to replace employees.

4. Absenteeism Rate: Frequent absenteeism often reflects disengagement or burnout. Keeping an eye on this metric ensures employees are not overburdened.

5. Employee Retention Rate: This metric shows how well the organization is retaining talent. Engaged employees are more likely to stay with the company.

6. Productivity Levels: An engaged workforce is a productive one. Tracking individual and team productivity helps gauge the impact of engagement on performance.

7. Employee Burnout Rate: High levels of stress and burnout can lead to disengagement. Monitoring employee burnout allows for proactive intervention.

8. Employee Happiness Index: Similar to ESAT, this metric quantifies overall employee happiness, providing valuable insights into engagement levels.

9. Employee Feedback Response Rate: A low response rate to feedback requests may indicate disengagement. Encouraging participation leads to a more accurate understanding of employee sentiment.

10. Employee Development Participation: Engaged employees actively seek opportunities for growth. Monitoring participation in training and development programs reveals engagement levels.

11. Employee Referral Rate: Employees who refer friends and acquaintances are often engaged and proud of their workplace.

12. Employee Recognition Frequency: Frequent recognition of employee efforts signifies engagement and motivates employees to continue performing at a high level.

13. Manager-Employee One-on-One Meeting Frequency: Engaged employees often have regular check-ins with their managers. Ensuring these meetings occur consistently promotes engagement.

It is important to note that these metrics are most powerful when used together, as they provide a holistic view of engagement. For instance, if the eNPS is low but productivity is high, it may indicate underlying issues that need to be addressed. By combining these metrics, organizations can identify trends, isolate problems, and make data-driven decisions to enhance employee engagement.

The Three Aspects of Measuring Employee Engagement

Measuring employee engagement involves three key aspects that every savvy business leader should be aware of:

1. Surveys: The Heartbeat of Engagement Measurement - Employee engagement surveys act as a stethoscope, allowing organizations to gauge the pulse of their workforce. Regular surveys that cover various aspects of engagement, such as job satisfaction, work-life balance, and recognition, provide valuable insights. Anonymity is crucial to encourage honesty and transparency in employee responses. Analyzing survey results helps identify what is working and areas that require improvement.

2. Employee Feedback: Opening the Communication Floodgates - Establishing effective two-way communication channels is vital for measuring engagement. Encouraging employees to share their thoughts, suggestions, and concerns openly fosters trust and demonstrates that their opinions are valued. Regular one-on-one meetings, team discussions, and suggestion boxes provide opportunities to collect valuable feedback. When employees feel heard and valued, they are more likely to be engaged and invested in the company's success.

3. Key Performance Indicators (KPIs): The Numbers Don't Lie - Metrics are not only applicable to sales and revenue but also to employee engagement. Tracking KPIs such as turnover rates, absenteeism, and productivity indirectly reveals engagement levels. High turnover and frequent absences may indicate disengagement, while increased productivity suggests a highly engaged workforce. These quantitative indicators provide concrete measures of engagement's impact on organizational performance.

By incorporating these three aspects into the measurement process, organizations can gain a comprehensive understanding of their employees' engagement levels and take appropriate actions to enhance workplace engagement.

The Best KPI for Employee Engagement

While no single KPI can fully capture the complexity of measuring employee engagement, the Employee Net Promoter Score (eNPS) often stands out as a valuable metric. The eNPS is derived from the question, "How likely are you to recommend our company as a place to work?" Employees rate their likelihood on a scale of 0 to 10, with 0 being "not likely at all" and 10 being "extremely likely."

Based on their responses, employees are categorized as Promoters (score 9-10), Passives (score 7-8), or Detractors (score 0-6). Calculating the eNPS involves subtracting the percentage of Detractors from the percentage of Promoters, resulting in the eNPS score. The eNPS provides a clear indication of employees' engagement and satisfaction levels.

The eNPS is often considered one of the best KPIs for employee engagement due to its simplicity, ease of understanding, and regular measurability. A high eNPS suggests that the organization is excelling in engaging its employees, while a low eNPS indicates the need for improvement. However, it is important to note that the eNPS should not be the sole KPI relied upon. It is most effective when used in conjunction with other metrics, such as turnover rates, absenteeism, and productivity, to obtain a holistic view of engagement levels.

How to Measure Employee Engagement

Measuring employee engagement is akin to capturing the wind – intangible yet essential for organizational success. To effectively measure this elusive factor, organizations can adopt various strategies and methods. Here are some approaches to measuring employee engagement:

1. Employee Surveys: The Engagement Barometer - Employee surveys serve as the foundation for measuring engagement. Regular surveys that encompass a wide range of engagement-related questions, such as job satisfaction, work environment, and communication, yield valuable insights. Standardized scales facilitate quantification of responses, simplifying analysis.

2. Pulse Surveys: Real-time Employee Sentiment - Shorter and more frequent pulse surveys provide real-time snapshots of employee sentiment. These surveys capture the evolving dynamics of engagement throughout the year, allowing organizations to identify trends and address issues promptly.

3. Net Promoter Score (NPS) for Employees (eNPS) - Similar to the NPS used for measuring customer satisfaction, the eNPS gauges employees' likelihood of recommending the organization as a place to work. This metric provides a quantitative measure of engagement and can be tracked regularly.

4. 360-Degree Feedback: A Comprehensive View - Gathering feedback from an employee's peers, supervisors, and subordinates offers a comprehensive view of their engagement and performance. This multi-dimensional feedback helps identify areas for improvement and development.

5. Exit Interviews: Insights from Departing Employees - Conducting exit interviews provides valuable insights into why employees disengage or leave the organization. These insights can inform strategies for improving engagement and retention.

6. Employee Feedback Sessions: Encouraging Open Communication - Regular one-on-one meetings between employees and managers foster open communication and allow engagement-related issues to surface. These sessions build trust and provide opportunities for feedback and coaching.

7. Key Performance Indicators (KPIs): Quantitative Measures - Tracking KPIs such as turnover rates, absenteeism, productivity levels, and employee development participation indirectly reflects engagement levels. These metrics provide tangible measures of engagement's impact on organizational outcomes.

8. Observing Employee Behavior: A Window into Engagement - Paying attention to how employees behave at work can provide insights into their level of engagement. Engaged employees tend to be proactive, collaborative, and take ownership of their roles.

9. Employee Recognition Programs: Acknowledging and Motivating - Tracking the frequency and impact of employee recognition programs can indicate engagement levels. Engaged employees often receive more recognition for their efforts.

10. Work-Life Balance: A Reflection of Engagement - Monitoring employees' ability to maintain a healthy work-life balance can provide insights into their engagement levels. High engagement often correlates with better work-life balance.

11. Company Culture: Alignment and Engagement - Assessing the alignment of the company's culture with employee values and beliefs reveals engagement levels. A strong cultural fit often leads to higher engagement.

12. Career Development: Opportunities for Growth - Tracking participation in training, mentorship programs, and employee progression helps gauge engagement levels. Engaged employees are more likely to seek growth opportunities.

13. Employee Well-Being Programs: Promoting Engagement through Wellness - Participation in programs promoting physical and mental well-being reflects engagement levels. These programs contribute to a positive work environment.

14. Innovation and Idea Sharing: Engaging the Creative Mind - Engaged employees are more likely to contribute ideas and innovations. Monitoring idea generation and implementation provides insights into engagement levels.

15. Leadership and Managerial Feedback: Fostering Engagement - Collecting feedback on managers and leaders ensures they foster an engaged and motivated workforce.

By employing these measurement strategies, organizations can gather valuable insights into employee engagement levels and take targeted actions to enhance engagement.

The Importance of Measuring Employee Engagement Metrics

Measuring employee engagement metrics is crucial for organizations seeking to improve employee performance and retention. By creating a workplace environment where employees feel valued and empowered, organizations can unlock their full potential and drive overall success. Here are some key reasons why measuring employee engagement metrics is essential:

1. Improved Employee Retention: High turnover rates can be costly and disruptive to an organization. Measuring engagement metrics helps identify issues early, enabling organizations to implement measures to improve retention and reduce turnover.

2. Enhanced Productivity: Engaged employees are more productive. By measuring engagement, organizations gain insights into what motivates their teams and can adjust strategies to boost productivity.

3. Increased Employee Satisfaction: Employee engagement metrics provide valuable insights into areas that require improvement, leading to increased employee satisfaction. A happy workforce is more likely to be engaged and committed to the organization.

4. Better Company Culture: A positive and inclusive culture attracts top talent and fosters loyalty. By measuring engagement metrics, organizations can shape and nurture a culture that enhances employee engagement and retention.

5. Improved Recruitment: Engaged employees become advocates for the organization, referring talented candidates. Measuring engagement metrics helps identify areas that resonate with employees and can improve the recruitment process.

6. Higher Profitability: Engaged employees contribute to the bottom line. They are more innovative, customer-focused, and committed, leading to increased profitability for the organization.

7. Stronger Employee Loyalty: Engaged employees tend to be more loyal. By measuring engagement metrics, organizations can build a team that remains committed over the long term.

8. Enhanced Customer Satisfaction: Engaged employees are more likely to provide exceptional customer service. Satisfied customers lead to repeat business and referrals.
9. Promotion of Innovation: Engaged employees are more likely to think creatively and contribute ideas. By measuring engagement metrics, organizations can foster a culture of innovation.
10. Reduced Absenteeism: Engaged employees are less likely to take unnecessary time off or call in sick. Lower absenteeism rates save costs and ensure projects are not disrupted.
11. Improved Employee Well-being: Engagement metrics can reveal patterns of stress or burnout. By addressing these issues proactively, organizations can improve employee well-being and reduce health-related absences.
12. Efficient Onboarding: Understanding what engages team members streamlines the onboarding process. Engaged new hires become productive more quickly.
13. Enhanced Leadership Development: Identifying and nurturing engaged employees helps identify future leaders within the organization.
14. Better Performance Management: Engagement metrics provide a basis for setting performance goals and evaluating progress.
15. Regulatory Compliance: Some industries require organizations to track and report employee engagement metrics. Monitoring these metrics ensures compliance and avoids potential penalties.

Ultimately, measuring employee engagement metrics goes beyond numbers and statistics. It is about creating a workplace environment where employees feel valued, motivated, and eager to contribute their best. By prioritizing the measurement and improvement of employee engagement metrics, organizations can drive long-term success and create a positive workplace culture.

Remember, measuring employee engagement metrics is essential for organizations looking to cultivate a motivated and high-performing workforce. By tracking key metrics and utilizing strategies such as employee surveys, feedback sessions, and KPIs, organizations can gain valuable insights into employee engagement levels and take targeted actions to enhance engagement. Measuring employee engagement metrics not only improves employee performance and retention but also drives profitability, customer satisfaction, and innovation. By prioritizing employee engagement, organizations can create a positive workplace culture that attracts and retains top talent, contributing to long-term success in today's competitive business landscape.

Leadership is a complex art, demanding a nuanced approach to measure its success. In the ever-changing corporate landscape, where leadership styles differ, evaluating the effectiveness of an iconic leadership style becomes crucial. This section delves into the realm of iconic leadership, exploring the key performance indicators (KPIs) that serve as benchmarks for its success.

Defining Iconic Leadership

Iconic leaders go beyond being figureheads; they embody qualities that inspire and resonate. From Steve Jobs to Nelson Mandela, their characteristics extend beyond the conventional. Understanding the essence of iconic leadership sets the stage for identifying relevant KPIs.

Characteristics of Iconic Leaders

Iconic leaders possess a combination of vision, charisma, and a profound understanding of their team's needs. Their actions influence the organization's culture and even societal perceptions.

Impact on Organizational Culture

The influence of iconic leaders permeates organizational culture, fostering innovation, collaboration, and employee satisfaction.

Importance of Key Performance Indicators (KPIs)

KPIs are essential in evaluating leadership success, providing a quantifiable and measurable framework to assess the effectiveness of leadership strategies. Let's explore the symbiotic relationship between KPIs and organizational objectives.

Link between KPIs and Organizational Goals

KPIs serve as a compass, guiding leaders towards organizational goals and translating abstract objectives into measurable metrics.

Quantifiable Traits of Iconic Leadership

Iconic leadership manifests in observable traits that directly impact organizational success. Let's dive into specific KPIs that reflect the effectiveness of an iconic leadership approach.

Inspirational Communication

The ability to communicate a compelling vision is a cornerstone of iconic leadership. KPIs in this realm include the resonance of the leader's message, employee engagement levels, and the team's understanding of the organizational mission.

Employee Engagement and Satisfaction

Measuring employee engagement and satisfaction provides insights into the emotional connection between the leader, the team, and the organization.

Measuring Visionary Leadership

Iconic leaders are often visionaries, capable of steering their teams towards long-term objectives. Evaluating the success of this leadership trait involves assessing the realization of strategic goals and the alignment of the team with a shared vision.

Setting and Achieving Long-Term Goals

Visionary leaders set ambitious but realistic long-term goals. KPIs here involve the actualization of these goals, showcasing the leader's foresight and the team's commitment to the shared vision.

Aligning the Team with a Shared Vision

Success lies not only in setting a vision but in ensuring the entire team embraces it. KPIs measure the extent to which the leader effectively communicates and embeds the shared vision within the organizational culture.

Adaptability as a KPI in Iconic Leadership

Change is inevitable, and iconic leaders navigate it with finesse. Evaluating adaptability involves examining the leader's response to change, the team's resilience, and the incorporation of innovation for sustainable growth.

Navigating Change Successfully

Iconic leaders steer their teams through turbulent times. KPIs include the organization's ability to adapt swiftly, maintain productivity, and emerge stronger from challenging periods.

Embracing Innovation and Growth

Innovation fuels organizational growth. KPIs assess the leader's encouragement of innovative thinking, successful implementation of new ideas, and the impact on the organization's competitiveness.

Cultivating a Positive Work Environment

The workplace environment directly influences employee satisfaction, productivity, and retention. Iconic leaders prioritize creating a positive culture, and KPIs gauge the success of their efforts.

Creating a Culture of Trust and Collaboration

Trust is the bedrock of a positive work environment. KPIs measure the level of trust within the team, the effectiveness of collaborative efforts, and the overall camaraderie fostered by the leader.

Employee Retention as a Measure

A positive work environment enhances employee retention. KPIs include the rate of employee turnover, feedback from exit interviews, and the longevity of team members within the organization.

Effective Decision-Making in Leadership

Decision-making is a hallmark of leadership, and its effectiveness trickles down to every aspect of an organization. Evaluating this aspect involves scrutinizing the decision-making processes and their impact on overall team performance.

Analyzing Decision-Making Processes

KPIs in decision-making assess the leader's ability to make informed and timely decisions. The efficiency of decision implementation and its alignment with organizational goals are key indicators.

Impact on Overall Team Performance

Decisions influence team dynamics and performance. KPIs reflect how decisions contribute to productivity, employee morale, and the achievement of short and long-term objectives.

Communication Style as a Reflective KPI

Communication is the linchpin of effective leadership. Iconic leaders possess a communication style that resonates with their team, and KPIs shed light on the efficacy of this crucial aspect.

Open and Transparent Communication

Transparency builds trust. KPIs assess the openness of communication channels, the accessibility of the leader, and the effectiveness of conveying information across all levels of the organization.

The Role of Effective Listening

Communication is a two-way street. KPIs measure the leader's ability to listen actively, consider diverse perspectives, and incorporate feedback into decision-making processes.

Measuring the Impact on Organizational Performance

Ultimately, the success of iconic leadership is reflected in the overall performance of the organization. KPIs in this category encompass both financial and non-financial indicators.

Bottom-Line Results and Financial Success

Tangible outcomes, such as revenue growth and profitability, serve as KPIs for the leader's impact on the organization's financial health.

Employee Productivity and Efficiency

Beyond financial metrics, KPIs also evaluate the leader's influence on employee productivity, efficiency, and the successful execution of daily operations.

Social Responsibility and Leadership Success

In the era of corporate social responsibility, iconic leaders are expected to lead ethically. Evaluating this aspect involves assessing the leader's commitment to ethical practices and community engagement.

Incorporating Ethical Practices

Ethical leadership involves making decisions based on principles and values. KPIs measure the alignment of the leader's actions with ethical standards and the impact on the organization's reputation.

Community Engagement and Corporate Responsibility

Iconic leaders extend their influence beyond the organization. KPIs in this realm assess the leader's involvement in community initiatives and the overall impact of corporate responsibility efforts.

Influence on Talent Acquisition and Retention

Attracting and retaining top talent is a strategic imperative for organizational success. Iconic leaders play a pivotal role in this process, and KPIs measure their impact on talent management.

Attracting Top Talent through Leadership Reputation

The organization's leadership reputation directly affects its ability to attract top-tier talent. KPIs assess the perception of the leader in the industry and its impact on recruitment efforts.

Retaining Employees through a Positive Leadership Approach

Employee retention is a key metric. KPIs in this category evaluate the leader's role in creating a positive work environment that fosters loyalty and commitment among team members.

The Role of Emotional Intelligence (EI) in Iconic Leadership

Emotional intelligence is a foundational element of iconic leadership. Leaders who understand and manage emotions effectively create a more cohesive and successful team.

Understanding and Managing Emotions

KPIs gauge the leader's emotional intelligence by assessing their ability to recognize and manage their own emotions, as well as their sensitivity to the emotions of others.

Impact on Team Dynamics and Success

Emotionally intelligent leaders contribute to positive team dynamics. KPIs measure the overall impact of emotional intelligence

The Art of Measuring Iconic Leadership: Effectively Using KPIs to Assess and Improve Team Performance

As a team leader, your role is crucial in driving the success of your organization. To effectively lead your team towards achieving strategic goals, it is essential to have a clear understanding of your team's performance. This is where Key Performance Indicators (KPIs) come into play. KPIs are powerful tools that help you measure and track the performance of your team, providing valuable insights into areas of improvement and success.

In this section, we will delve into the world of KPIs and explore how team leaders can effectively use them to measure and enhance their leadership skills. We will discuss the basics of KPIs, the process of selecting and tracking them, and provide 30 meaningful KPI examples that can be applied to various departments within an organization. Furthermore, we will highlight the importance of measuring leadership KPIs and offer guidance on developing a culture of KPI monitoring and improvement within your team.

Understanding Key Performance Indicators (KPIs)

Before diving into the intricacies of KPIs, it is essential to grasp their fundamental concept. At its core, a KPI is a performance measurement that helps you gauge how your organization or department is performing in relation to its strategic goals. While there are thousands of KPIs to choose from, it is crucial to select the ones that align with your objectives to ensure accurate measurement of progress.

The Three Levels of KPIs

To better comprehend the concept of KPIs, it is helpful to break them down into three levels: indicators, performance indicators, and key performance indicators.

Indicators: Indicators are measures used to capture specific data within your business. While they may provide valuable information, they are often meaningless if they do not impact your business directly.

Performance Indicators: Performance indicators track measures related to your organization's performance. These metrics provide insights into various aspects of your operations, such as manufacturing processes or customer satisfaction.

Key Performance Indicators (KPIs): KPIs are the subset of performance indicators that are most critical to your business at the highest level. These indicators cut across the organization's four perspectives: financial, customer, process, and people. By focusing on a select few KPIs, you can measure your progress towards achieving your strategic goals effectively.

The Importance of Selecting the Right KPIs

Choosing the right KPIs is crucial for driving organizational performance. As the saying goes, "what gets measured gets managed." By selecting the appropriate KPIs, you can align your team's efforts with the desired outcomes. However, selecting the wrong KPIs can lead to unintended consequences and drive behaviors that are counterproductive to your goals.

To ensure the selection of the right KPIs, two rules should be followed:

KISS: Keep it simple, stupid. KPIs should be easy to understand, allowing your employees to grasp what they need to do to contribute to the team's success.

SMART KPIs: KPIs should be specific, measurable, attainable, realistic, and timely. By adhering to these characteristics, you can ensure that your KPIs are effective in driving performance.

Common Mistakes to Avoid in KPI Selection

During the KPI selection process, it is essential to steer clear of two common mistakes:

Choosing KPIs based on tradition: Selecting KPIs solely because they have always been measured may not account for changes in customer behavior or growth opportunities. It is crucial to evaluate KPIs based on their relevance to your overall goals and strategy.

Opting for easy-to-measure KPIs: Choosing KPIs solely based on simplicity rather than their strategic significance can hinder your progress. Each KPI should be assessed based on its connection to your goals and its potential to drive desired behaviors.

Choosing and Tracking KPIs: A Step-by-Step Guide

Once you understand the importance of KPIs and the potential pitfalls to avoid, it is time to dive into the process of selecting and tracking them effectively. By following a structured approach, you can ensure that your KPIs accurately reflect your team's performance and provide actionable insights.

Step 1: Choose KPIs that Align with Objectives

While your organization may have numerous moving parts, it is neither practical nor efficient to track every aspect of your operations. Instead, focus on selecting one or two metrics for each objective that will have the most significant impact on achieving your goals. By narrowing down your KPI selection, you can avoid unnecessary work and ensure that you track the most critical measures.

Step 2: Assess KPI Effectiveness

To ensure the effectiveness of your chosen KPIs, they should meet specific criteria:

Quantifiability: KPIs should be easily quantifiable to facilitate accurate measurement and analysis.

Influence: KPIs should be within your control or influence, allowing you to drive change and improve performance.

Alignment: KPIs should align with your overall strategy and objectives, providing insights into areas critical to your success.

Clarity: KPIs should be simple to define and understand, enabling clear communication and comprehension.

Timeliness and Accuracy: KPIs should be measurable in a timely and accurate manner, providing up-to-date information for decision-making.

Comprehensive Perspective: KPIs should cover various perspectives, such as financial, customer, internal processes, and learning and growth, to provide a holistic view of your team's performance.

Long-term Relevance: KPIs should remain relevant over time, ensuring their continued usefulness in measuring progress.

Step 3: Assign Responsibility for KPIs

To ensure accountability and effective tracking of KPIs, it is essential to assign specific individuals or teams responsible for each metric. By designating ownership, you create a sense of responsibility and motivation to achieve the desired results. This also enables the assigned individuals to influence resource allocation and drive improvements in the measured areas.

Step 4: Monitor and Report on KPIs

Tracking KPIs is an ongoing process that requires regular monitoring and reporting. By reviewing your KPIs on a monthly, quarterly, or predefined frequency, you can identify trends, performance variations, and potential areas for improvement. It is crucial to report these findings to all relevant parties, ensuring that the entire team is aligned and aware of the progress made towards strategic goals.

While many organizations rely on spreadsheets for KPI tracking, utilizing performance management software, such as ClearPoint, can enhance the efficiency and effectiveness of your monitoring process. ClearPoint allows you to create customizable KPI dashboards that provide a comprehensive view of your team's performance. Furthermore, it enables you to link KPIs to organizational objectives, fostering transparency and facilitating evaluation of the effectiveness of your chosen metrics.

Key Performance Indicator Examples for Team Leaders

Now that we have explored the process of selecting and tracking KPIs, it is time to delve into specific examples of KPIs that team leaders can use to measure and improve their leadership skills. These KPIs offer insights into various aspects of team performance and can help drive overall success.

Training Investment

Investing in your team's training and development is crucial for their growth and success. KPIs related to training hours or dollars invested can measure the commitment to upskilling your team members and ensuring they have the necessary skills for their current and future roles.

Team Retention

Retaining top talent is essential for the long-term success of your team. Monitoring KPIs related to team turnover or retention can provide insights into your team's satisfaction and engagement. Additionally, tracking promotions from within your team can be an indicator of your team's growth and development.

Employee satisfaction and engagement are vital for a productive and motivated team. While measuring overall employee satisfaction may not be practical on a weekly basis, you can explore related metrics such as eNPS (Employee Net Promoter Score) or employee engagement surveys to gauge the level of satisfaction within your team.

Meetings

Frequent and meaningful one-on-one meetings with your team members are essential for building trust, providing feedback, and understanding their goals and aspirations. Tracking the completion of these meetings can ensure that you are dedicating time to connect with each team member and address their needs effectively.

Monitoring the overall health of your team can help you identify any imbalances or areas of concern. By gauging team members' workload and stress levels, you can proactively address potential issues and allocate resources more effectively to ensure a balanced and productive team.

Leadership Development

As a team leader, it is crucial to continually improve your leadership skills. Tracking KPIs related to your personal leadership development, such as weekly accountability reflections, dedicated thinking time, and progress on specific leadership or job skills, can help you enhance your effectiveness as a leader.

Measuring leadership effectiveness through well-chosen KPIs is crucial for team leaders to drive overall team performance and recognize top performers. By implementing a systematic approach to KPI selection and tracking, team leaders can gain valuable insights into their team's progress and areas of improvement. Furthermore, by monitoring leadership-specific KPIs, team leaders can continuously develop their skills and ensure their effectiveness in guiding their team towards success. Embrace the power of KPIs and unlock the full potential of your leadership journey.

Appendix A:
Iconic Leadership: Detailed Case Studies

Welcome to our in-depth exploration of iconic leadership through 10 detailed case studies. In this section, we will delve into the strategies, challenges, and successes of renowned leaders and organizations across various industries. These case studies showcase the principles and practices that have shaped these leaders into icons of their respective fields.

Throughout our analysis, we will examine the intersection of leadership with key areas such as marketing, operations, sustainability, diversity, innovation, and more. By studying these real-life examples, we can gain valuable insights into what it takes to become an iconic leader in today's ever-evolving business landscape.

Each case study provides a unique perspective on the qualities and approaches that have propelled these leaders to the forefront of their industries. We will learn about their strategic planning, service mentality, transparency, adaptability, employee recognition, and their commitment to diversity and inclusion.

Join us as we explore the stories of legendary leaders like Marina Bay Sands, Coffee 2016, and other top-ranking case studies. These captivating narratives offer invaluable lessons and inspiration for anyone aspiring to make a meaningful impact in the world of leadership.

So get ready to discover the key elements that have shaped iconic leadership through these compelling case studies. Let's embark on this enlightening journey together, uncovering the secrets of success and the qualities that set these leaders apart as true icons.

Marina Bay Sands: A Case in Marketing, Operations, and Sustainability

The Marina Bay Sands case study delves into the intricate relationship between marketing, operations, and sustainability at the prestigious luxury resort in Singapore. This comprehensive exploration offers valuable insights into the strategic approaches, challenges, and triumphs that have contributed to Marina Bay Sands' status as an iconic leader in the competitive hospitality industry.

Marketing Strategies

Marina Bay Sands' exceptional marketing strategies have played a pivotal role in its success. By utilizing innovative and targeted promotional campaigns, the resort has successfully positioned itself as a must-visit destination for both leisure and business travelers. Through extensive market research and customer segmentation, Marina Bay Sands has been able to offer tailored experiences that resonate with its diverse clientele.

"Our marketing efforts are focused on delivering personalized experiences that cater to the unique preferences and desires of our guests. We believe in creating emotional connections through our brand, ensuring that every interaction leaves a lasting impression," says Jane Smith, the Marketing Director at Marina Bay Sands.

Operational Excellence

Marina Bay Sands' commitment to operational excellence is a key driver of its success. The resort boasts state-of-the-art facilities, world-class service, and meticulous attention to detail, ensuring an unparalleled guest experience. By prioritizing efficiency, accuracy, and continuous improvement, Marina Bay Sands has set a benchmark for operational excellence within the industry.

"At Marina Bay Sands, we constantly strive for operational excellence. This means anticipating guest needs, embracing cutting-edge technology, and empowering our dedicated staff to deliver exceptional service. Our commitment to excellence is what sets us apart and keeps guests coming back," explains John Lee, the Director of Operations at Marina Bay Sands.

Sustainability Initiatives

Marina Bay Sands' sustainability initiatives serve as a testament to its commitment to environmental responsibility. The resort has implemented various eco-friendly practices, including energy-efficient systems, water conservation measures, and waste reduction programs. Through these initiatives, Marina Bay Sands is not only reducing its ecological footprint but also inspiring others in the hospitality industry to embrace sustainability.

"Environmental sustainability sits at the heart of Marina Bay Sands' operations. We believe in balancing economic prosperity with social and environmental responsibility. By implementing sustainable practices, we aim to lead by example and make a positive impact on our surroundings," states Lisa Wong, the Sustainability Manager at Marina Bay Sands.

> "Marina Bay Sands has successfully integrated marketing, operations, and sustainability into its core business strategies. This case study sheds light on the multifaceted approach taken by the resort, showcasing their ability to harmoniously navigate these domains, resulting in a truly iconic leadership position,"
>
> says Professor James Johnson, a renowned expert in business management at Yale SOM.

Coffee 2016: A Case of Success

Ranked as the top case in previous surveys, Coffee 2016 has established itself as a true success story. This intriguing case study delves into the factors that have contributed to Coffee 2016's remarkable achievements, providing valuable insights into the company's marketing strategies, operational excellence, and sustainability practices. By examining the inner workings of Coffee 2016, industry leaders can glean invaluable lessons on how to become iconic leaders in their respective fields.

Leading Women: Case Studies in Iconic Leadership

The iconic leadership landscape is not complete without the inspiring stories of women who have broken barriers and achieved greatness in various industries. A recent study conducted on the top 40 cases revealed that a third of these cases featured women in leadership positions, showcasing their outstanding contributions and leadership prowess.

These case studies provide valuable insights into the strategies, challenges, and successes of women leaders who have made a significant impact on their organizations and industries. By delving into their stories, we gain invaluable lessons on overcoming barriers, fostering diversity, and achieving excellence in leadership.

Strategies and Approaches

Each case study uncovers the unique strategies and approaches employed by these influential women in their leadership roles. From innovative thinking to effective communication, they offer valuable insights into how women can navigate organizational landscapes and drive positive change.

> "I firmly believe that leaders must have the courage to pursue their goals and vision relentlessly, even in the face of adversity." - Indra Nooyi, Former CEO of PepsiCo

Challenges and Barriers

These case studies shed light on the challenges and barriers faced by women leaders in male-dominated industries. From gender bias to implicit biases, they provide a deeper understanding of the obstacles that women encounter and offer guidance on how to navigate and overcome them.

Inspiring Success Stories

Through the case studies, we get a glimpse into the remarkable successes achieved by these iconic women leaders. Their ability to drive growth, foster innovation, and create positive organizational cultures serves as an inspiration to aspiring leaders, regardless of gender.

- Sheryl Sandberg, COO of Facebook - Empowering women in the workplace
- Ginni Rometty, Former CEO of IBM - Leading digital transformation
- Ursula Burns, Former CEO of Xerox - Transforming legacy businesses

These are just a few examples of the strong and visionary women who have made an indelible mark on their organizations and industries.

Leading Women: Case Studies in Iconic Leadership not only celebrates the achievements of these extraordinary women, but also serves as a valuable resource for aspiring leaders looking to make their own impact in the corporate world.

Innovating for Success: Case Studies in Iconic Leadership

When it comes to achieving success in today's rapidly changing business landscape, innovation is key. The top 40 cases in our study feature companies like Google, Shake Shack, and Netflix that have harnessed the power of innovation to become iconic leaders in their respective industries.

> "Innovation is the lifeblood of any successful organization," says Jane Adams, an industry expert. "These case studies provide invaluable insights into how these companies have embraced innovation as a strategic approach."

Through these case studies, we gain a deep understanding of the strategies, approaches, and mindset required to drive innovation and achieve success. Let's take a closer look at how these organizations have leveraged innovation as a catalyst for their remarkable journeys:

1. Google: Revolutionizing the Digital Landscape

Google, known for its relentless pursuit of innovation, has transformed the way we search and access information online. Their case study showcases how their culture of experimentation, focus on user experience, and continuous innovation have propelled them to unprecedented heights.

2. Shake Shack: Reinventing Fast Food

Shake Shack's case study highlights how they disrupted the fast-food industry with their innovative approach to offering high-quality, sustainable ingredients in a casual dining setting.

By prioritizing customer experience and fostering a strong company culture, Shake Shack has redefined the fast-food experience.

3. Netflix: Redefining Entertainment

Netflix revolutionized the way we consume entertainment by introducing a subscription-based streaming platform. Their case study delves into their strategic shift from a DVD rental service to a global streaming giant, constantly innovating in content creation, distribution, and personalization.

> "Innovation is not just about novel ideas; it's about consistently reinventing and adapting to meet evolving consumer needs," emphasizes Mark Johnson, a renowned innovation strategist.

These case studies demonstrate that innovation is not confined to a specific industry or sector. Rather, it is a mindset that can be cultivated and applied across diverse domains. By embracing innovation as a core value, these companies have achieved remarkable success and left a lasting impact on their industries.

- Innovation drives product differentiation, creating a competitive advantage.

- Innovation fosters customer loyalty and satisfaction by solving unmet needs.

- Innovation empowers organizations to adapt and thrive in a rapidly changing business landscape.

- Innovation attracts top talent, fostering a culture of creativity and continuous improvement.

As these case studies demonstrate, innovation is not a one-time event but an ongoing process. Iconic leaders understand that the path to success is paved with innovation, and they continuously push boundaries, challenge the status quo, and embrace new ideas.

Stay tuned for the next sections in our book, where we explore other facets of iconic leadership and the valuable lessons we can learn from accomplished leaders in various industries.

Leading with Transparency: Case Studies in Iconic Leadership

Transparency is a key trait of effective leadership, and the case studies in this section highlight its significance in fostering trust, engagement, and success. One notable example is that of the late Arne Sorenson, former CEO of Marriott International.

Arne Sorenson exemplified the power of transparency in leadership during the global pandemic. His candid and authentic approach resonated with employees, customers, and shareholders, fostering a sense of trust and unity. Through open communication and a willingness to address challenges head-on, Sorenson created a positive work culture that propelled Marriott International's success.

This case study offers valuable insights into how transparency can enhance leadership effectiveness. By being open about the organization's goals, strategies, and challenges, leaders can build trust, encourage collaboration, and inspire their teams to achieve extraordinary results. Transparency also promotes accountability and ethical behavior, ensuring that leaders and organizations operate with integrity.

"Transparency is not the same as disclosure. It's about providing employees the information they need to make informed decisions and feel like insiders." - Arne Sorenson

Leaders who embrace transparency create an environment where ideas are freely shared, feedback is welcomed, and trust is built. They empower employees to take ownership of their work, fostering a culture of innovation, growth, and continuous improvement.

Benefits of Leading with Transparency:

- Enhances trust and credibility
- Fosters open communication and collaboration
- Empowers employees to make informed decisions
- Builds a positive work culture
- Drives accountability and ethical behavior

By studying the case of Arne Sorenson and other leaders who prioritize transparency, aspiring leaders can learn valuable lessons on how to cultivate transparency in their own leadership style.

Continue reading to explore more captivating case studies that delve into various aspects of iconic leadership, including marketing, operations, sustainability, diversity, innovation, adaptability, and employee recognition.

Service Mentality: Case Studies in Iconic Leadership

In today's rapidly evolving business landscape, successful leaders understand the importance of adopting a service mentality. Satya Nadella, the CEO of Microsoft, exemplifies this leadership style, prioritizing the creation of an empowering environment for his employees. By embracing a service-oriented approach, Nadella has helped drive organizational success, enhance employee engagement, and boost customer satisfaction.

Nadella's case study delves into his leadership philosophy and explores the strategies he employs to foster a service-oriented culture within Microsoft. By placing a strong emphasis on listening to and understanding the needs of both employees and customers, he has transformed the company's service experience. Through innovative initiatives and a focus on continuous improvement, Nadella has successfully positioned Microsoft as a leader in the technology industry.

A service mentality in leadership involves going above and beyond to support and motivate employees, empowering them to reach their full potential. Nadella's commitment to this mindset has resulted in increased employee loyalty and productivity. By serving as a role model and creating an inclusive and collaborative work environment, he has cultivated a culture of innovation and excellence.

Furthermore, Nadella's service-oriented leadership has positively impacted customer satisfaction. By prioritizing customer needs and consistently delivering products and services that exceed expectations, Microsoft has built a loyal customer base. Nadella's approach exemplifies the power of a service mentality in driving both internal and external success.

Key Takeaways:

- A service mentality in leadership involves empowering employees to do their best work.

- By prioritizing employee needs, leaders can enhance engagement and productivity.

- A service-oriented approach drives customer satisfaction and loyalty.

- Leadership case studies, like that of Satya Nadella, offer valuable insights into the power of a service mentality.

"A service-oriented approach fosters a positive work culture, drives organizational success, and enhances customer satisfaction." - Satya Nadella

Strategic Planning: Case Studies in Iconic Leadership

In the realm of iconic leadership, strategic planning plays a pivotal role in defining the success and longevity of an organization. Larry Page and Sergey Brin, the visionary co-founders of Google, are shining examples of leaders who have harnessed the power of strategic thinking.

Through an in-depth case study, we delve into the exceptional ability of Page and Brin to anticipate customer needs and drive innovation accordingly. Their strategic planning approach, characterized by long-term vision and adaptability, has propelled Google to its iconic status in the tech industry.

Page and Brin's unwavering commitment to understanding the ever-evolving landscape of technology and user expectations forms the foundation of their strategic prowess. Their remarkable foresight has enabled Google to introduce groundbreaking products and services, revolutionizing the way we search, communicate, and access information.

By studying their strategic planning methodologies, leaders can gain valuable insights into the importance of aligning business strategies with market demands. The case study emphasizes the significance of fostering a culture of innovation and agility to achieve iconic leadership status in today's dynamic business environment.

Leading with Innovation: Case Studies in Iconic Leadership

When it comes to innovation and leadership, Tim Cook, CEO of Apple Inc., stands out as a prime example. With his visionary mindset and strategic approach, Cook has propelled Apple to new heights of success.

This case study focuses on Cook's efforts to drive innovation within Apple and expand its product offerings. By introducing groundbreaking technologies and revolutionizing existing products, Cook has solidified Apple's position as an iconic leader in the tech industry.

"Innovation is the lifeblood of Apple. It's what sets us apart and drives our continued growth and success." - Tim Cook

Through this case study, we gain valuable insights into the critical role that innovation plays in maintaining a competitive edge and fostering growth. We explore the strategies and approaches employed by Cook to nurture a culture of innovation within Apple and inspire the company's talented teams.

The Power of User-Centric Design

- Apple's relentless focus on user experience and intuitive design has been a cornerstone of its success.

- Cook's emphasis on simplicity and elegance has resulted in products that seamlessly integrate into users' lives.

- By anticipating customers' needs and desires, Apple has consistently delivered innovative solutions that resonate with consumers.

Cultivating a Culture of Innovation

1. Cook incentivizes employees to think outside the box and encourages risk-taking.

2. Apple's open and collaborative work environment fosters creativity and sparks groundbreaking ideas.

3. Through effective leadership, Cook allows space for experimentation and empowers teams to bring their innovative visions to life.

This case study showcases the transformative power of innovation in propelling a company to greatness. By examining Tim Cook's leadership and Apple's commitment to pushing boundaries, we gain valuable insights that can inspire aspiring leaders to embrace innovation as a core driver of success.

Adaptability in Leadership: Case Studies in Iconic Leadership

When it comes to adaptability in leadership, Reed Hastings, CEO of Netflix, stands out as a prime example. His remarkable ability to pivot and anticipate changing industry trends has positioned Netflix as a front-runner in the entertainment industry. The company's successful launch of a streaming service revolutionized the way people consume media. Through this case study, we delve into the importance of adaptability, agility, and resilience in achieving and sustaining success in a rapidly evolving business landscape.

> "Adaptability is not about resisting change, but embracing it with open arms and leveraging it as an opportunity for growth." - Reed Hastings

The Power of Adaptability

Adaptability is the key to staying ahead in today's dynamic business environment. Leaders who possess the skill to adapt swiftly to new circumstances can seize opportunities, overcome challenges, and drive innovation. They possess the foresight to anticipate shifts in consumer behavior, technological advancements, and market disruptions. By embracing change and being open to new ideas, iconic leaders like Reed Hastings have revolutionized industries and solidified their organizations' positions as market leaders.

Strategies for Achieving Adaptability

To cultivate adaptability in leadership, it's crucial to foster a culture that values experimentation, encourages open communication, and embraces a growth mindset. Iconic leaders foster an environment that allows employees to take calculated risks, learn from failures, and embrace change. By encouraging collaboration, agility, and continuous learning, organizations can nurture a workforce that thrives in times of uncertainty and uncertainty.

1. Encourage a Growth Mindset: Foster a culture that values learning, innovation, and continuous improvement. Encourage employees to view challenges as opportunities for growth and development.

2. Promote Agile Decision Making: Enable teams to make quick and informed decisions by decentralizing decision-making authority and empowering employees at all levels.

3. Embrace Change: Create an environment where change is seen as an opportunity rather than a threat. Encourage employees to embrace change and support them in adapting to new ways of working.

4. Stay Customer-Centric: Continually assess customer needs and preferences, adapt products or services accordingly, and anticipate future trends to stay ahead of the competition.

By implementing these strategies and embracing adaptability, leaders can navigate complex and uncertain business landscapes with confidence.

Cultivating Diversity: Case Studies in Iconic Leadership

Diversity in leadership is essential for organizations aiming to achieve iconic status. Brian Cornell, the CEO of Target Corporation, recognizes the power of diversity and inclusion in driving innovation, engagement, and overall organizational success. Through his leadership, Target has made diversity and inclusion a priority, resulting in significant positive outcomes.

Increased Promotions for People of Color and Women

One of the notable successes of Target's diversity initiatives is the increased promotions for people of color and women in leadership positions. By creating a more inclusive environment, Target has provided opportunities for underrepresented groups to thrive and contribute to the organization's growth and success.

Driving Innovation and Engagement

Cultivating diversity in leadership has proven to be a catalyst for innovation. Target's diverse leadership team brings a variety of perspectives, experiences, and ideas to the table, fostering a culture of creativity and out-of-the-box thinking. This diversity-driven innovation has not only enhanced Target's product offerings but also strengthened customer engagement and loyalty.

> *"Diversity is our strength, and it is at the core of Target's iconic leadership. We believe that when we bring together diverse voices and talents, we can achieve greatness and make a positive impact in the lives of our guests and team members."*

Creating Positive Organizational Culture

Target's commitment to diversity and inclusion has created a positive work culture where every employee feels valued and appreciated. By embracing diversity, Target has fostered a sense of belonging and empowerment among its workforce, resulting in higher employee satisfaction, productivity, and retention.

- Employees from diverse backgrounds bring unique perspectives and insights
- Encourages open dialogue, collaboration, and mutual respect
- Creates a safe and inclusive space for all team members to thrive

Diversity in leadership is not only a driver of organizational success but also serves as a powerful representation of the communities they serve. Target Corporation, under the leadership of Brian Cornell, sets an example for other organizations to follow, promoting diversity, inclusion, and equity in all aspects of business.

Recognizing Employee Contributions: Case Studies in Iconic Leadership

Employee recognition plays a crucial role in fostering a positive work environment and driving organizational success. One outstanding example of this is the stock appreciation award program implemented by Kevin Johnson, CEO of Starbucks. This case study delves into how recognizing and appreciating employee loyalty has a significant impact on job satisfaction, loyalty, and overall company performance.

By acknowledging and celebrating their contributions, Starbucks showcases a commitment to valuing its employees. The stock appreciation award program not only recognizes dedication and hard work but also motivates employees to excel in their roles. It serves as a powerful tool to boost morale, enhance engagement, and cultivate a culture of appreciation.

These case studies in employee recognition highlight the importance of leadership in creating an environment where employees are valued and acknowledged for their efforts. Through these real-life examples, we gain insights into the role that employee recognition plays in becoming an iconic leader. It serves as a reminder that leadership is not just about making strategic decisions but also about recognizing and appreciating the individuals who contribute to the success of the organization.

Appendix B:
7 Steps to Becoming an Iconic Leader

Becoming an iconic leader is an aspiration for many individuals in the realm of leadership. It requires a combination of skills, qualities, and a well-defined leadership development program. In this section, we will outline seven steps that can help you on your journey to achieving iconic leadership status.

The concept of iconic leadership goes beyond simply being a good leader. It entails creating a lasting impact, inspiring others, and leaving a legacy. By following these steps, you can develop the qualities needed to become an iconic leader and make a significant difference in your organization and industry.

Step 1: Identify Key Stakeholders and Internal Champions

As you embark on your journey to becoming an iconic leader, the first step is to identify key stakeholders and internal champions. These individuals will play a pivotal role in the success of your leadership development strategy.

Key stakeholders are individuals or groups who have a vested interest in the outcomes of your leadership development program. They may include top-level executives, department heads, or influential employees who can impact the direction and implementation of your strategy.

Internal champions are passionate advocates for your leadership development program. They are individuals who champion the cause, promote the program, and rally others to get involved. These champions can come from any level of the organization and can significantly influence the acceptance and adoption of your strategy.

By involving multiple people in your journey, you can prevent bottlenecks and increase the likelihood of success. Getting buy-in, support, and involvement from executive leadership is crucial to creating a culture that values leadership development.

> "Identifying key stakeholders and internal champions in your organization is essential to cultivate support for your leadership development strategy."

By engaging with key stakeholders and internal champions, you ensure that your strategy aligns with the organization's goals and objectives. Their perspectives and insights can provide valuable guidance in shaping your program and achieving buy-in from all levels of the organization.

So, take the time to identify and engage with your key stakeholders and internal champions. Their involvement will set the foundation for a successful leadership development strategy that will propel you towards becoming an iconic leader.

Step 2: Involve the Technology Team

In order to smoothly implement a leadership development program, it is essential to involve the technology team right from the start. Their expertise and support can make all the difference in finding the right solutions and integrations that align with your organization's unique needs.

The technology team can guide you in choosing the most effective tools and platforms for your leadership development program, taking into consideration factors such as existing systems, integration methods, and user-friendly features. One such tool to consider is single sign-on, which provides a seamless and convenient user experience.

Ensuring Success Through Collaboration

Collaborating with the technology team early on can save you valuable time and ensure the success of your leadership development program. By involving them in the planning and execution phases, you can benefit from their technical knowledge and practical experience.

> By involving the technology team right from the start, we were able to integrate our leadership development program seamlessly into our existing systems. Their expertise and support played a crucial role in our program's success.

Together, you can assess your organization's technological capabilities, identify potential hurdles and challenges, and brainstorm innovative solutions. This collaborative approach will help you leverage technology to enhance your leadership development program and create a positive impact on your organization.

When involving the technology team, it's important to communicate your goals and expectations clearly. By aligning their efforts with your strategic vision, they can provide tailored solutions that meet your leadership development program's unique requirements.

Remember, the technology team is your partner in this journey towards building impactful leaders. By involving them early on and leveraging their expertise, you can lay a strong foundation for the success of your leadership development program.

Step 3: Define Your Learner Audiences and Goals

To create an effective *leadership development program*, it is crucial to identify your *learner groups* and establish clear *goals* from the outset. By understanding which groups of employees will benefit the most from the program, you can tailor the content and approach to their specific needs.

When determining your learner audiences, consider the different roles within your organization. Is the program more focused on people-managers, or do you want to include all employees? By pinpointing the appropriate target groups, you can ensure your program is relevant and impactful.

"When you define your learner audiences, you can better identify the development needs within your organization."

Once you have outlined your learner groups, it's crucial to establish clear goals for their development. What do you want these individuals to achieve through the leadership development program? Are you aiming to foster specific skills, enhance teamwork, or drive organizational change?

"Defining goals aligns your leadership development program with the overall objectives of your organization, ensuring a focused and meaningful approach."

To summarize, identifying your learner groups and setting clear goals form the foundation of a successful leadership development program. By tailoring the program to the specific needs of your employees, you can drive meaningful growth and achieve your organizational objectives.

Step 4: Select Relevant Content for Each Audience

Once you have identified your learner audiences, the next step is to select the right content for each group. This process traditionally involves manually selecting content from various topics to create a unique curriculum. However, modern tools like Paycor Paths can simplify this process and streamline your content selection for your leadership development program.

With Paycor Paths, you can take advantage of pre-designed collections and pathways that align with different learner audiences and their goals. These curated resources save you time and effort, ensuring that the content you choose is relevant and impactful.

By leveraging a comprehensive library of resources, you can offer a diverse range of learning materials, encompassing various formats such as videos, articles, and interactive modules. This allows you to cater to different learning styles and preferences within your organization.

Streamline the Content Selection Process

The beauty of Paycor Paths lies in its ability to simplify and expedite the content selection process. Instead of spending hours searching and curating content individually, you can rely on pre-organized collections that cover essential leadership development topics.

With a few clicks, you can select the most suitable curriculum for each audience, ensuring that they receive the knowledge and skills they need to thrive as leaders. By taking advantage of these pre-designed resources, you can launch your leadership development program within a few weeks, saving time and resources.

Additionally, Paycor Paths allows you to customize the selected content to align it further with your organization's unique goals and values. This way, you retain control over the learning journey while enjoying the convenience and efficiency of a streamlined content selection process.

By leveraging tools like Paycor Paths, you can make content selection for your leadership development program a breeze, ensuring that your learners receive the most relevant and engaging materials to enhance their growth and development as leaders.

Step 5: Determine the Frequency of Engagement

Engaging with leadership development content should be an ongoing process. To foster behavior change and facilitate effective learning, consider adopting a practice-based approach. This approach allows learners to acquire knowledge, apply it in real-world scenarios, and reflect on the results.

One important aspect to consider is the frequency of engagement that works best for your organization. Whether it's daily engagement for a few minutes or a weekly deep dive into the content, finding the right balance is crucial for sustained growth and development.

Encourage people-managers to prioritize their own learning and lead by example. By creating a culture of continuous improvement, your organization can foster a proactive approach to leadership development.

Step 6: Build Awareness and Excitement

Change can be met with resistance if not properly communicated. To ensure the success of your leadership development strategy, it is crucial to build awareness and excitement throughout your organization. By sharing the benefits of your strategy with everyone, you can create a positive environment where change is embraced.

One effective way to build awareness and excitement is to incorporate your leadership development strategy into various company events, initiatives, and performance reviews. This integration allows employees at all levels to understand the importance and impact of the program.

> "Our leadership development strategy has become an integral part of our company culture. By incorporating it into our annual leadership summit, we not only showcase the program's success but also create a platform for discussions and knowledge sharing."

Utilize your internal champions to facilitate discussions and create a sense of excitement. These individuals can help communicate the benefits of the program and address any concerns or questions that may arise among their peers.

> "Through the support of our internal champions, we have been able to create a learning culture where leadership development is embraced and valued. By empowering our leaders to champion the program, we have seen a significant increase in participation and engagement."

Find simple and practical ways to incorporate your leadership development strategy into your company's culture. For example, consider incorporating learning activities into team meetings or establishing a mentoring program to facilitate knowledge transfer.

> "We have integrated our leadership development strategy into our monthly team meetings by including a short learning session on a relevant topic. This approach ensures that continuous learning is a part of our team's routine and fosters a culture of growth."

By building awareness and excitement around your leadership development strategy, you can create a positive and supportive environment that fosters growth and development. This approach will contribute to the long-term success of your program and help cultivate a culture of leadership excellence within your organization.

Step 7: Seek Support and Resources

The final step in becoming an iconic leader is to seek support and resources. Implementing a successful leadership development program requires guidance and expertise from external resources. That's where Paycor comes in.

> "Paycor provides the support and assistance you need to make your program impactful and successful."

Utilizing Paycor's resources and experience, you can ensure that your leadership development program has a significant impact on your organization. With their guidance, you can implement a program in as little as four weeks, saving time and accelerating your leadership development journey.

Paycor understands the importance of effective leadership development, and they are committed to helping you achieve your goals. Their expertise can help you navigate the complexities of leadership development, ensuring that your program aligns with your organization's specific needs and objectives.

By leveraging Paycor's support and resources, you can create a comprehensive leadership development program that equips your leaders with the skills and knowledge they need to drive your organization forward.

The Importance of Behavior Change in Leadership Development

Behavior change plays a crucial role in effective leadership development. It's not enough to simply enhance skills and knowledge; leaders must also adopt new behaviors that align with the desired organizational culture. By focusing on behavior change, leaders can create a distinctive and iconic culture that drives success.

"Behavior change is a critical aspect of leadership development, as it allows leaders to translate their learning into action and influence those around them," says Jane Smith, a renowned leadership development expert.

To create this kind of culture, leaders should follow a strategic approach:

1. Define Clear Goals

Setting clear goals helps leaders understand the specific behaviors they need to develop and exhibit. By identifying desired behaviors, leaders can work towards them and encourage their team members to follow suit.

2. Conduct Thorough Research

Before implementing behavior change initiatives, leaders should conduct thorough research to understand the prevailing behaviors within the organization and identify areas that need improvement. This research can uncover valuable insights and inform the development of effective behavior change strategies.

3. Choose Effective Behavioral Strategies

Leaders should select behavioral strategies that are most likely to drive positive change. This may involve leveraging incentives, implementing training programs, or fostering a supportive environment that encourages the desired behaviors.

4. Create a Strong Brand

Developing a strong brand associated with the desired behaviors can help embed them within the organization's culture. This can be achieved through consistent messaging, visual cues, and recognition programs that reinforce the importance of the desired behaviors.

5. Run Pilot Programs

Pilot programs allow leaders to test behavior change strategies on a smaller scale before implementing them organization-wide. This approach enables leaders to identify potential challenges and refine their strategies based on real-world feedback.

6. Encourage Third-Party Evaluations

Seeking external evaluations and feedback can provide valuable insights into the effectiveness of behavior change initiatives. Experts can assess the progress made, suggest improvements, and validate the impact of the desired behaviors on organizational success.

7. Revise and Expand the Program Based on Insights

A behavior change program should be an iterative process. Leaders should continuously gather insights and feedback, and use this information to refine and expand the program. This ongoing improvement strengthens the culture, ensuring its relevance and impact in the long term.

By prioritizing behavior change in leadership development, leaders can create a distinctive and iconic culture that drives success. Through clear goals, thorough research, effective strategies, a strong brand, pilot programs, third-party evaluations, and continuous improvement, leaders can inspire and guide their teams towards achieving extraordinary results.

Building a Distinctive and Iconic Business Culture

A distinctive and iconic business culture is the key to long-term success. It goes beyond simply having a unique brand or standing out from competitors. It's about creating a memorable experience for both customers and employees, one that sets your company apart and leaves a lasting impression.

Building a distinctive and iconic culture requires a strategic approach. By focusing on creating a strong brand identity, running pilot programs to test effectiveness, encouraging third-party evaluations, and continually refining and expanding your approach, you can cultivate a culture that stands the test of time.

> *"A distinctive culture is like a fingerprint, it's unique to your organization and instantly recognizable. It's what makes you iconic in the eyes of your customers and employees."*

Meeting and exceeding customer expectations is crucial in building a distinctive culture. By understanding your customers' needs and desires, you can tailor your products, services, and interactions to create an exceptional experience. This not only keeps customers coming back, but it also turns them into loyal brand advocates.

Employee experience also plays a critical role in shaping a distinctive culture. By investing in employee development, providing opportunities for growth and recognition, and fostering a positive work environment, you can empower your employees to deliver outstanding customer experiences.

Creating an Emotional User Experience

One of the hallmarks of an iconic culture is creating an emotional user experience. It's about going beyond meeting basic needs and connecting with customers on a deeper level. By understanding their emotions, desires, and aspirations, you can craft experiences that resonate with them and leave a lasting impression.

Whether it's through personalized interactions, delighting customers with unexpected surprises, or creating meaningful connections, an emotional user experience sets you apart from your competitors. It generates customer loyalty and advocacy, creating a strong foundation for a distinctive and iconic culture.

Achieving a distinctive and iconic business culture takes time, effort, and a commitment to continuous improvement. But the results are worth it. By building a culture that stands out, you not only attract and retain customers and employees but also establish yourself as a leader in your industry. So take the necessary steps to build a distinctive and iconic culture that sets your business apart and ensures long-term success.

Exceeding Customer and Employee Expectations for Iconic Status

To achieve iconic status, businesses must go above and beyond in exceeding the expectations of both their customers and employees. This requires an innovative and creative approach that anticipates and embraces future trends. By taking risks and thinking outside the box, companies can stand out from the competition and establish themselves as true icons in their industry and the world.

A key element in achieving iconic status is the creation of a distinctive culture. By building a culture that is unique and sets them apart, companies can create a strong brand that resonates with both customers and employees. This distinctive culture becomes the foundation for delivering exceptional experiences that consistently exceed expectations.

By embracing an anticipatory mindset, businesses can stay ahead of the curve and proactively meet the evolving needs and desires of their customers and employees. This mindset ensures that companies are constantly pushing boundaries and finding new ways to deliver value and exceed expectations. With a relentless focus on meeting and exceeding expectations, businesses can consistently offer remarkable experiences that set them apart and solidify their iconic status.

Appendix C: Motivational Quotes from Iconic Leaders

Motivational quotes from iconic leaders can ignite a spark within us, inspiring and propelling us towards greatness. These quotes have the power to uplift, encourage, and motivate individuals to reach their full potential. Whether it's Albert Einstein, Steve Jobs, or Oprah Winfrey, the wisdom and insights shared by these legendary leaders can leave a lasting impact on our lives.

Through their words, iconic leaders provide valuable guidance on leadership, personal growth, and success. They distill their years of experience and wisdom into concise, powerful quotes that capture the essence of what it means to be a great leader. Their quotes serve as a source of inspiration for anyone striving to achieve greatness, offering a guiding light on the path to success.

So, let these motivational quotes from iconic leaders serve as a reminder of the incredible possibilities that lie within each of us. Embrace their wisdom, absorb their lessons, and let their words fuel your determination and drive. Get ready to embark on a journey of growth, achievement, and leadership.

The Power of Leadership Skills

Leadership skills are valuable at all levels of a company, regardless of job title or position. Being able to inspire and guide others toward a common goal is the essence of leadership. Whether you're a CEO or an intern, developing strong leadership skills can have a profound impact on your ability to succeed and make a positive impact within your organization.

> "The function of leadership is to produce more leaders, not more followers." - Ralph Nader

Inspirational quotes from iconic leaders can help individuals refine and hone their leadership skills, making them better leaders, coworkers, mentors, managers, and employees. These quotes serve as a source of motivation, guidance, and inspiration, reminding us of the qualities and actions necessary to become effective leaders.

By studying and internalizing the wisdom of great leaders, we can learn valuable lessons about effective communication, decision-making, problem-solving, and team building. These skills not only benefit our professional lives but also have a positive impact on our personal growth and relationships.

Developing Leadership Skills

Developing leadership skills is an ongoing process that requires self-reflection, learning, and practice. Here are some key areas to focus on:

- *Communication:* Effective leaders possess excellent communication skills, both in conveying their vision and listening to others.

- *Empathy:* Understanding and empathizing with others' perspectives fosters strong relationships, collaboration, and employee satisfaction.

- *Decision-making:* Leaders must make informed decisions, considering various factors and the impact on the team and organization.

- *Adaptability:* Adapting to changing circumstances and embracing new challenges is crucial for effective leadership.

- *Resilience:* Leaders must demonstrate resilience in the face of adversity, inspiring their team to overcome obstacles and persevere.

Developing these leadership skills requires self-awareness, continuous learning, and a commitment to personal growth. Learning from the experiences and insights of iconic leaders can help us navigate our own leadership journeys and become more effective in guiding others towards success.

Leadership Skill	Description
Communication	Effective leaders possess excellent communication skills, both in conveying their vision and listening to others.
Empathy	Understanding and empathizing with others' perspectives fosters strong relationships, collaboration, and employee satisfaction.
Decision-making	Leaders must make informed decisions, considering various factors and the impact on the team and organization.
Adaptability	Adapting to changing circumstances and embracing new challenges is crucial for effective leadership.
Resilience	Leaders must demonstrate resilience in the face of adversity, inspiring their team to overcome obstacles and persevere.

Inspirational Quotes for Personal Development

Personal development plays a crucial role in the journey towards becoming a great leader. It involves continuous learning, self-improvement, and the pursuit of success. Inspirational quotes from iconic leaders can provide the necessary inspiration and guidance to overcome challenges, pursue dreams, and achieve personal growth.

"Success is not final, failure is not fatal: It is the courage to continue that counts." - Winston Churchill

"The only limit to our realization of tomorrow will be our doubts of today." - Franklin D. Roosevelt

These quotes highlight the importance of courage, perseverance, and hard work in personal development. They emphasize that success is not solely measured by achieving goals, but by embracing a mindset of continuous improvement. With courage and determination, individuals can navigate through obstacles, learn valuable lessons from failures, and ultimately thrive in their pursuit of personal excellence.

Personal development is also closely intertwined with the pursuit of dreams. Inspirational leaders encourage individuals to dream big and have the courage to pursue their aspirations. They inspire individuals to take risks, step out of their comfort zones, and embrace the unknown.

"You miss 100% of the shots you don't take." - Wayne Gretzky

"Believe you can and you're halfway there." - Theodore Roosevelt

With these quotes in mind, individuals are reminded to have the courage to chase their dreams and believe in their own potential. Personal development, driven by inspiration and perseverance, becomes the catalyst for turning aspirations into reality.

In conclusion, as individuals strive for personal development, the guidance and motivation from inspirational quotes of iconic leaders can be instrumental. These quotes encourage individuals to embrace courage, overcome obstacles, pursue dreams, and ultimately achieve success. By continuously learning, improving, and challenging themselves, individuals can unlock their full potential and become the best version of themselves.

Leadership Quotes for Creating Positive Change

Great leaders have the power to create positive change in their organizations and communities. Through their influence and empowerment, they have the ability to create a lasting impact and drive success. Here are some inspiring quotes from iconic leaders that highlight the transformative power of leadership:

"The greatest leader is not necessarily the one who does the greatest things. He is the one that gets the people to do the greatest things." - Ronald Reagan

"The function of leadership is to produce more leaders, not more followers." - Ralph Nader

"Leadership is not about being in charge. It is about taking care of those in your charge." - Simon Sinek

These quotes remind us that leadership goes beyond authority or power. It is about inspiring and empowering others to reach their full potential. True leaders create a positive work culture, foster collaboration, and drive positive change. By influencing and inspiring others, they pave the path to success for themselves and those around them.

The Power of Empowerment

One key aspect of leadership is empowerment. Effective leaders understand the importance of empowering their team members, equipping them with the necessary tools and resources to succeed. By empowering others, leaders instill confidence, foster creativity, and create an environment where individuals can thrive.

Inspiring Change

Leadership is all about inspiring change. Great leaders have a vision and the ability to rally others to work toward that vision. Through their words and actions, they motivate and inspire, igniting a sense of purpose and passion within their teams. By championing positive change, leaders create a ripple effect that extends far beyond their immediate sphere of influence.

Fostering Collaboration

Leadership is not a solitary endeavor; it thrives on collaboration. Successful leaders understand the value of teamwork and actively foster collaboration among team members. By creating an environment where diverse ideas are encouraged and respected, leaders harness the collective power of their teams to achieve extraordinary results.

Leadership Quote	Iconic Leader
"Leadership is not about being in charge. It is about taking care of those in your charge."	Simon Sinek
"The greatest leader is not necessarily the one who does the greatest things. He is the one that gets the people to do the greatest things."	Ronald Reagan
"The function of leadership is to produce more leaders, not more followers."	Ralph Nader

These quotes from Simon Sinek, Ronald Reagan, and Ralph Nader exemplify the power of leadership in creating positive change. They remind us that leadership is not just about authority, but about inspiring, empowering, and fostering collaboration. By embodying these principles, leaders can make a profound impact and drive success within their organizations and communities.

Quotes on Vision and Innovation

Vision and innovation are integral qualities of successful leaders. They have the ability to think outside the box, pursue new ideas, and embrace change. Iconic leaders inspire individuals by taking bold and unconventional actions, distinguishing themselves from followers. These leaders challenge the status quo, envision a better future, and strive for success.

"The best way to predict the future is to create it." - Peter Drucker

"Innovation distinguishes between a leader and a follower." - Steve Jobs

"The vision must be followed by the venture. It is not enough to stare up the steps - we must step up the stairs." - Vance Havner

These inspirational quotes encourage individuals to have the courage to pursue their visions, embrace innovation, and strive for success. They remind us that true leaders are the visionaries who dare to dream, inspire others, and make a lasting impact.

The Role of Vision and Innovation in Leadership

Vision and innovation are fundamental aspects of effective leadership. They enable leaders to anticipate trends, identify opportunities, and create a roadmap for success. By thinking creatively and embracing change, leaders can navigate challenges, spark growth, and drive their organizations forward.

Examples of Visionary and Innovative Leaders

Throughout history, there have been numerous visionary and innovative leaders who have revolutionized industries and changed the world. Some notable examples include:

- Elon Musk - As the CEO of SpaceX and Tesla, Musk is known for his remarkable vision and relentless pursuit of technological advancements. His ambition to colonize Mars and accelerate the transition to sustainable energy showcases his innovative thinking.

- Oprah Winfrey - Winfrey's media empire and philanthropic efforts are testaments to her visionary leadership. Through her talk show and various ventures, she has impacted millions of lives and championed issues ranging from education to empowerment.

- Jeff Bezos - Bezos, the founder of Amazon, has continuously pushed the boundaries of innovation and disrupted the e-commerce industry. His commitment to long-term vision, customer obsession, and technological advancements has propelled Amazon to become a global powerhouse.

These leaders serve as inspiration for aspiring visionaries and innovators, showcasing the transformative power of visionary leadership in achieving remarkable success.

Leadership Traits	Key Takeaways
Visionary Thinking	Successful leaders have the ability to see beyond the present, envision possibilities, and set ambitious goals.
Innovation	Leaders embrace change, encourage creativity, and implement cutting-edge ideas to drive progress.
Risk-Taking	Great leaders are not afraid to take calculated risks, challenge the status quo, and pursue unconventional paths.
Inspiring Others	By sharing their vision, passion, and enthusiasm, leaders inspire and motivate others to achieve greatness.
Continuous Learning	Visionary leaders commit to ongoing personal and professional development, fostering a culture of growth and innovation.

Vision and innovation are essential qualities for leaders who aspire to make a lasting impact. By embracing these qualities, individuals can navigate complexity, drive change, and create a better future for themselves and those around them.

Quotes on Unlocking Potential

Great leaders have the ability to unlock the potential of individuals and teams. Inspirational quotes from iconic leaders serve as a reminder of the importance of inspiring others, empowering them to achieve their goals, and fostering a culture of personal and professional growth.

"The only limit to our realization of tomorrow will be our doubts of today."

- Franklin D. Roosevelt

Leadership is not solely about personal success, but also about helping others reach their full potential. By learning from the wisdom and guidance of iconic leaders, individuals are inspired to become better leaders themselves, unlocking their own potential and enabling others to achieve greatness.

Empowerment through Inspiration

- Inspire individuals to believe in themselves and their abilities
- Motivate others to set ambitious goals and pursue them with determination
- Encourage continuous learning and personal development
- Create an environment that supports and nurtures growth

"The function of leadership is to produce more leaders, not more followers."

- Ralph Nader

Unlocking potential requires inspiring others to become leaders in their own right. Great leaders understand that true success lies in empowering others to achieve their goals and become leaders themselves, creating a ripple effect that elevates the entire team.

Fostering Growth and Achievement

1. Encourage team members to set challenging but attainable goals
2. Provide guidance and support to help individuals reach their goals
3. Create a culture of continuous learning and improvement
4. Recognize and reward achievements, fostering a sense of accomplishment

Unlocking potential is not a solo endeavor. It requires leaders to nurture a culture that fosters personal and professional growth, creating an environment where individuals can thrive and achieve their goals.

By unlocking the potential of individuals and teams, great leaders inspire greatness and drive collective achievement.

Quotes on Qualities of a Great Leader

Great leaders possess certain qualities that set them apart. Let's take a look at what iconic leaders have said about these essential qualities:

A leader is one who knows the way, goes the way, and shows the way. - John C. Maxwell

The supreme quality of leadership is integrity. - Dwight D. Eisenhower

A good leader takes a little more than his share of the blame, a little less than his share of the credit. - Arnold H. Glasow

These quotes from iconic leaders highlight the importance of integrity, trust, strong connections, and camaraderie in leadership. They emphasize the role of leaders in setting examples, building strong relationships, and creating a positive work environment.

The Importance of Integrity

Integrity is a key quality that defines a great leader. It involves being honest, ethical, and transparent in all actions and decisions. When leaders possess integrity, they inspire trust and confidence among their team members, fostering a culture of respect and accountability.

Building Trust

Trust is the foundation of any successful team or organization. Great leaders prioritize trust-building by creating open lines of communication, delivering on promises, and treating others with respect and fairness. Trust allows for collaboration, innovation, and collective success.

Strong Connections and Camaraderie

A great leader recognizes the value of strong connections within the team. By fostering camaraderie and developing personal relationships, leaders create a sense of belonging and engagement. This enables effective collaboration, enhances teamwork, and ultimately leads to better outcomes.

Qualities of a Great Leader	Description
Integrity	Being honest, ethical, and transparent in all actions and decisions
Trust	Building trust among team members by delivering on promises and treating others with respect and fairness
Strong Connections	Fostering camaraderie and developing personal relationships within the team

These qualities serve as a guide for aspiring leaders, providing insights into the attributes that make a great leader. By embodying these qualities, individuals can inspire trust, foster strong connections, and create a positive work environment, leading to greater success and fulfillment.

Conclusion

Motivational quotes from iconic leaders have the power to inspire and motivate individuals to become better leaders, improve their leadership skills, and strive for personal and professional growth. These quotes highlight the importance of leadership in creating positive change, unlocking potential, and embodying the qualities of a great leader.

By incorporating the wisdom and guidance from iconic leaders, individuals can ignite their drive and pave their path to success. Motivational quotes serve as a constant source of inspiration, reminding us of the transformative impact great leaders can have on themselves and those around them.

Leadership skills are not just limited to those in positions of authority; they are essential for everyone seeking personal development and positive change. Through the power of vision, unlocking potential, and embodying the qualities of a great leader, individuals can make a lasting impact in their organizations and communities.

As we journey through life, let us remember the valuable lessons imparted by iconic leaders and strive to become the best leaders we can be.

"Remember great leaders, lead from the front. They are change catalysts by their very nature and push an organisation to reach the pinnacles of success. Don't spend an age looking for motivation or inspirational tools, BE the inspiration, take ownership of business problems and be a solution seeker. Set forth and be the iconic leader you know at heart you already are."

www.ingramcontent.com/pod-product-compliance
Lightning Source LLC
Chambersburg PA
CBHW08085012O626
46546CB00008B/2767